FAMILY CAMP

S'MORE THAN A VACATION

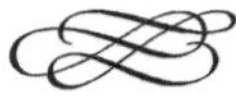

MARIA WARNER

CAMP VALUES THAT CREATE
HAPPY HEALTHY FAMILIES

A mother helps her family (and herself) reset their values after the shock of 9/11 by introducing them to the family camp way of life.

CHARITY

All proceeds from book sales will go to:
Ed and Dottie Hecker Scholarship Fund

(The Ed and Dottie Hecker Scholarship Fund provides financial assistance to families in need so they can participate in Deer Valley programs including summer camp.)

ACKNOWLEDGMENTS

My family has been immeasurably supportive in this effort. One thing writing has provided me is thick skin. Mike, Michael, Mia, and Megan have kept me authentic. Thank you!

Susan Pohlman, my coach, walked this journey with me the entire way. Nadine Kenney Johnstone, a new addition to my efforts, and all the writers mentioned in the book also carved out space to nurture this effort. My beta readers have their own projects, families, and work, and yet they still made time to guide me. Thank you, Anne Wilson, Hope Dougherty, Miriam Aliberti, and Susan Chlebowski.

And of course, all the alumni who camped with me, and those that will hopefully carry on this tradition for another fifty years, or more. Keep the family camp spirit in your heart!

To everyone who listened to me talk about this and probably wondered how a book could take five-plus years to write—it's finished! Let's celebrate! Milkshake, anyone?

My parents introduced me to the family camp experience forty-plus years ago. When my father died, my brother Scott said, "We should have his service the same morning as we would have left for camp. That week each year was one of the happiest of his life." It's one of the best weeks for me and my family, too. Thank you, Mom and Dad! You have taught me the importance of "taking care of one another."

INTRODUCTION

In 2016, I picked up a pen and decided to write book. I had never written one before, but I felt compelled to put our family's story on the page. Our personal story of a family lost to a family found. From a family overwhelmed by schedules, sports, work, technology, and extra-curricular activities to one that embraced simplicity and family values. From a family that spent hours apart to one that found a way to reconnect with each other and nature.

How did we do that? We made a commitment to spend a week at a family camp every summer. It changed our lives in many deep ways and continues to do so to this day. Family camp is so much more than just a week in the woods. It is a time to remember who we are as individuals, who we are as a family, and who we are as citizens of the earth. It is a week to laugh, love, and grow together.

Brene Brown, PhD, MSW says, "Loving ourselves through the process of owning our story is the bravest thing we'll ever do." I love this story, our story. I hope you do too. If you can get even one nugget of an idea that you can use at home to make your family healthier and happier, then I will know that the courage it took to write this memoir was worth it. I believe that all families would benefit from going to a family camp. If that isn't possible, then bring some of the camp ways into your home. I promise you'll be glad that you did!

LIFE BEFORE FAMILY CAMP

Mike and I met at the University of Pittsburgh and built a life together. Several moves for his career and three children in a span of four years found us living in New Jersey. Mike busied himself starting a new company while I filled every minute of our time with activities that the top-selling books told me would make us a successful family. Sports, music, religious education, and scouts kept us running after school and on the weekends.

While this may have worked for a family with lots of support, it wasn't working for us. Mike's long commute into New York City kept him away from home until late into the evening. His business travel meant days without his extra set of hands to help drive, cook, or to give me a break. I hired an au pair to live with us and help with the kids and chores, but that didn't seem to lessen the amount of stress we were experiencing. I should have recognized that our pace was unsustainable when our son, Michael, refused to get in the car for his piano lesson, Mia locked her bedroom door when it was time for church, and Megan asked for Leonie, the au pair, to kiss her ouchie instead of me. Oh, and the girls were wearing sandals with socks instead of closed-toe shoes because I didn't have time to take them shopping.

We used their lack of proper footwear as an excuse to take Mike's car service into Manhattan. After shopping, he took us up to his office on the 102nd floor of the World Trade Center to enjoy the view. Looking out, a quarter mile above street level, I saw the sparkling city stretch north. We were on top of the world, and I acted like it, too. I had come to expect the au pair, the limo rides, and buying the children stuff. Coming a long way from my scraping quarters together in college, I had bought into the idea of making money as a measure of success. It all seemed worth it at the time. Mike's long workdays and the constant activity that led to rebellious behavior from the kids were part of life, right?

To look for ways to squash the kids' rebellious behaviors, I bought more books on parenting. I assumed the next "expert" had the answers for the one right way to raise a family. One day I realized I was *reading* how to be the best family instead of *being* one. I had lost my way by replacing my ideals with junk values. The hard truth that we needed to change our lifestyle wouldn't be delivered via a book. No, that lesson came on September 11, 2001.

Instead of Mike heading into the office that morning, he prepared to catch a flight to a board meeting in San Francisco. He never caught that plane as they were all grounded after the terrorists struck the towers. Our loss of a sense of security was engulfing. Dear friends perished along with cherished coworkers. The kids had classmates whose parents died. Needing to protect ourselves from the sorrow settling like the gray ash of the collapsed towers, I tossed the calendar into the garbage. Everything was canceled except for our attendance to funerals. Driving to each wake on the weekends, Mike and I had time for deep reflection. Life had fallen apart. We needed to start over. This was our wake up.

Our conversations in the car led to the decision for Mike to sell the company and give us the time and space we needed to regroup as a family. Thoughts of how we planned to lessen our load kept me hopeful.

After the sale and the transition period, Mike's noncompete gave us the opportunity we had hoped for to slow down and reconnect. We took the kids to the Jersey Shore, Arizona to visit Mike's parents, and Pittsburgh to see mine. The family time was important for us, but after a conversation with my mom and dad, I had more direction.

"We really got off track and sideways, Mom."

"How so?"

"I got caught up reading every bestseller on how to create the perfect family, and Mike got wrapped in work."

"Maria, I read there are five times as many parenting books out now as a decade ago," Mom said. "All the advice is overwhelming."

"We never needed any books," Dad said. "We just went to family camp."

"I want to give the kids more than camping," I said.

"But camp is so much more!" Mom said.

"You'll be able to focus on the values that make for a great family," Dad said.

Huh, maybe they were right. As a kid, my family had attended the same camp each summer for many years. There was something about family camp that kept us concentrating on positive principles instead of junk ideals like how many activities your kids were involved in or what label was on your clothing. My family had struggled when my siblings and I were in our teen years.

Sitting in my parents' living room, I thought about my childhood. There was an argument every night. The TV was too loud, "someone" left the lights on, the last brownie was eaten by "wasn't me," all of which led to yelling. Seeking to avoid confrontation, I made myself super busy. I swam after school and had a different extracurricular activity every night to minimize time at home. My community became everyone but family.

During that time, my dad's childhood friend, Al,

shared family camp details with my parents. He explained how the YMCA designed events for fun and to build connections. Al insisted it was a wonderful place to get support from other adults, too. Shortly after their conversation, my parents introduced swapping our beach vacation for camp.

Going to camp became our go-to vacation and a way for us to deepen our relationships. Time together, nature, and community, plus other benefits helped us bond. After we started going to camp, we became more considerate, played cards, and included one another in ice cream runs. I had forgotten about the joy of camping together as a family.

Perhaps family camp would be the answer for us too. It was worth a try.

THE DECISION

As Mike and I drove home, I reminded him of my childhood family camp experience. The kids were occupied watching a movie in the backseat—which was good because I didn't want them to overhear. They were tired and looking forward to being at home and sleeping in their own beds.

"Remember the fall foliage weekend you and I went to in the woods years ago?" I asked.

"Yeah, at the camp with the lake and hiking trails?"

"Yup, well, my parents suggested we go as a family."

"I thought you said it's really hard to clear the wait list." He was right. Most families returned annually, and it was difficult to find an opening.

"Well, I called and put our name on the list, and we're next in line."

"Okay, this is the summer to do it if we can get in."

"I know. You'll be returning to work soon."

For the rest of the car ride, I thought about how we had done a really good review of our work-life balance. The company was sold, and yet, I was still pulled to scheduling every aspect of our world—in my search for what? I believed it was up to me at this point to revisit this camp idea. I could lean on the camp administration's expertise with families to guide me in our new path.

We pulled into our driveway. The hatch of the Dodge Grand Caravan lifted, bags unzipped, and Mike fed dirty laundry right into the washer. Grabbing their Huffy bikes, the kids peeled out of the driveway. Entering the kitchen, I answered the ringing telephone. I held my hand over the receiver and called Mike.

"Who is it?" he asked.

"Camp is calling," I said.

"Who?" he asked again.

"It's family camp," I said. "They have an opening."

"So fast? You just signed up."

"I know, what do I tell them?"

"Let's do it."

"We haven't even unpacked." I looked at our full trunk.

"Say yes, we'll figure it out later."

I was surprised we cleared the list. Anticipating we would be bumped to the following year, I thought I had the time I needed to prepare the kids. Mike and I were going to have a battle with them as we had promised them no more travel. School was just around the corner. I knew they looked forward to being at home.

Over dinner, the kids overflowed with the happenings of the neighborhood. As they spoke of sleepaway invitations, I realized we'd better not delay informing them of the change in our schedule.

"Mom, my buds missed me," Michael said.

"I bet they did." I looked at Mike willing him to share the news.

"Get all your fun over the next four days!" he said.

"Why?" asked Megan.

"Cause then we're off to the camp Mom went to as a kid."

"What?" Michael said, "No!"

"I want my buddies," he said. "Haven't we had enough family time?" At eleven years old, he had done a remarkable job of dealing with his younger sisters all summer. I knew how much he wanted to hang with his friends.

"At camp, you'll be with kids your age," I said. It didn't work. His face reddened with anger.

"We don't want to go to some camp you went to as a girl," Mia said. Three years younger than Michael, our previously quiet daughter had become talkative. Lately, we had started hearing her thoughts on everything, and I do mean everything. She crossed her arms and sat back in her chair.

"Are there bugs?" Megan asked. Biting insects left

welts on every inch of her skin. Glancing between us, she nibbled her lower lip.

Making eye contact with Mike, my look said *we are really pushing it.*

"We'll coat you with bug spray," he said. "As for you two…we're going."

"I loved it as a kid and I hope you do too," I said.

Just like my siblings and me when my parents informed us we were going to camp, the kids ran, crying, to their bedrooms. Their doors banged. Crack! I sighed. How do you explain to spoiled children that another vacation is just what they needed? Hoping that my parents were right, I needed to trust their wisdom. I loaded the plates into the dishwasher. Mike returned to the laundry room and folded the clean clothes right back into our duffels.

Pausing at each of their doors on my way to bed, I listened for sniffles. Not hearing any, I snuggled into my side of the bed. As I drifted to sleep, I hoped they'd appreciate camp as much as my family had all those years ago.

The next morning, I wrote my list of to-do items. At the top was talking to Mom. I wanted to thank her for prompting my call to camp. And second was letting my best friend Jenni know we had cleared the wait list. She had attended with me as a child. I hoped she had called the office to put her family on standby. How great would it be for us to raise our kids together at camp!

WELCOME TO FAMILY CAMP

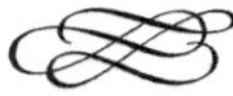

<u>Saturday Arrival</u>

Four days later, the kids begrudgingly scrambled into our white minivan and settled in their seats. Hitting the Pennsylvania turnpike, we rolled by farm after farm. After the kids had seen enough cows, they turned to their electronics. This would be their final chance. Once we arrived, everyone would have to leave their devices behind. No exceptions. Camp was a tech-free zone.

After two hours we exited the freeway and wound through the country towns of Western Pennsylvania.

"There's a buggy." Michael pointed to an Amish family.

"Look at all those windmills," Megan added. (Future Sustainability Studies Major)

"The road's so windy!" Mia said. She was correct; they followed the streams.

"Turn right at the twin silos," I said. Providing instructions based on landmarks I recalled from years ago, I helped Mike navigate the unmarked roads. Not much had changed since my last visit.

"There's a candy shop and a hand-fashioned chair store," I said.

Turning at each marker built my anticipation. When we reached the highest point of elevation in the state, Mt. Davis, I knew we were there.

"Look for deer," I said. As a youngster, one greeted my family at the entrance sign. When I had told the story to our kids, they hoped for their own deer reception.

Reaching the entry, a different creature greeted us. Staff! Dressed in costumes—wizards, superheroes, and pirates—they yelled, "Hello! Welcome!" while blowing whistles and waving their arms.

I leaned out the window and high fived them as we drove by. The smell of mountain air, pine, and earthiness flowed into the car. Each inhale filled me with the essence of camp and every exhale pushed away the outside world. I was back.

Mike parked and the kids scrambled to escape. The office lawn was the spot where everyone connected.

They quickly joined a gaggle of kids kicking a soccer ball.

Leaving them to play, we went into the paneled office to finalize our payment. Cindy, the office coordinator, took my credit card. "Welcome back, Maria! Is this your homecoming?"

"Yup, it's been fifteen years. This is my husband, Mike, and our kids are outside."

"Let me check my list. There's Michael, age eleven, and Mia and Megan, both eight years old. Are they twins?"

"Megan is a little younger than Mia," I said.

"She's adopted from China," Mike said.

"Well, we have a few adoptive families," Cindy said. "You'll fit right in."

"I remember," I said. "Everyone is made to feel they belong."

"Here you go." She handed me my Visa, along with our lodging and meal assignment. She offered Mike the activity list and name tags.

"Horseback riding, volleyball, sailing lessons, and bocce ball," Mike said. "I'm doing all of these."

"Hey, remember we're trying to rebalance our lives?" I said. "Don't wear yourself out."

"Or you'll need another vacation," Cindy said. We laughed as we were vacationed out, but we knew this was a once-in-a-lifetime summer. Once Mike returned to work, travel would be limited. We wanted to capture a new way of being as a family. We wanted to use this opportunity to set that course and become the nourishing family we had intended all those years ago.

"No worries. Tonight, I'll be organizing my entire week." He smacked the rolled papers into his hand for emphasis.

I smiled at Cindy, and she winked. We both knew every first-year camper made this mistake. I too had raced from one activity to the next when I was young, trying to squeeze in as much as possible. I rode horses in the morning, practiced volleyball before lunch, sailed in the afternoon, and played cards in the evening before tumbling into bed. I ended my week exhausted, napping every afternoon. He would have to learn this for himself.

"We're assigned to the same cabin I stayed in with my family," I said.

The girls had befriended sisters. It was excellent to see returning campers still reaching out to the newcomers. It reminded me of the school assembly, *No One Eats Alone*, where a single person reached out to someone new, subsequently creating a culture of belonging and a whole movement. This was exactly what I hoped the kids learned. Not to be friends with someone because they had the trendiest toy, but to appreciate them for their character. Such as these young ladies' kindness.

We corralled them to leave the lawn long enough to unpack. Weaving up the hill into the massive oak trees heavy with leaves, we turned right on the dirt road.

Navigating the car around large protruding rocks, Mike stopped at number twelve. It was the same as I remembered. The painted sides were a dark utilitarian brown, green moss grew on the roof, and the porch sagged a little in the middle from years of use. We traversed the rickety steps onto the wood deck. The hinges of the screen door squeaked as I tugged it open.

"Nothing has changed! It's the same," I said. I was thrilled by this revelation. Consumed with my return, I wanted everything to be as I remembered.

Our living space would be six hundred square feet. There were two bedrooms separated by a powder room. Pointing to the room with the double bed, I said, "See, the parents get the full bed, and the kids are on the other side with single bunks."

The kids dragged their bags to their side. I heard them discussing the merits of the top bunk versus the bottom. Michael acquiesced to the girls and let them have their choice—upper beds.

"Where's the shower?" Mike asked. He stared at the powder room separating our bedrooms.

I pointed to the wash house. "I packed bath caddies and flip-flops for everyone."

Walking around, he wiped dust off a shelf. "This is pretty rustic…" He shot me a look.

"It's fantastic! We'll be dirty, and no one will care," I said.

"Rachel and Becca invited us to their cabin," Megan said. Gripping Mia's hand, she pulled her out the door.

I hoped Michael would make a friend soon, so he would stop being angry at me.

Michael called, "Can I go and make a friend?"

"Go ahead, I'll unpack."

Turning to Mike I asked, "You okay to take the car to the parking lot without me?"

"There's a path through the woods back to the office, right?" he asked. He remembered from our fall foliage weekend.

"I'm looking forward to not having to drive this week," I said.

"Yup! Our own bubble from the rest of the world."

Everyone left me. I rolled out the children's sleeping bags and fluffed their pillows. There were three shelves, one per kid. I laid their clothes out. Placing their toothbrushes on the sink, I paused and thought—how simple. Everything they needed for the week; they didn't need electronics, designer clothing, or expensive experiences.

Returning, Mike organized his shelf. "Do you need any help?" he asked.

"No thanks, I'm enjoying how this reminds me of my parents and siblings."

"Okay, I'm going for a walk to get reoriented," Mike said. "It's been years since you brought me here."

"I'll meet you at the song circle."

The door shut behind him, and I had the entire cabin to myself. Moving to our bed, I placed the event list on the nightstand. Camp smelled the same, the dirt, pine trees, crushed leaves. I tucked our pillows at the headboard and decided to lie down and reminisce. My mind replayed memories of my father unpacking our cherry red wagon as my mother swept cobwebs from the corners. I hoped this calling to return to camp took seed in my husband and kids. Though hopeful, I did not, at the time, really understand the depth of what we had put in motion—a new family tradition.

A tradition that I hoped provided comfort and stability. Something that we had all missed since 9/11. I longed for certainty. Considering that the cabins hadn't changed assured me camp would be a familiar place, providing a comfortable environment in which to explore meaningful values. I thought I am exactly where I'm meant to be.

In what seemed like only minutes, the ringing of the dinner bell brought me out of my reverie. I knew the sound was the signal for campers to gather at the sing-along area. Closing the door on my childhood, I left the cabin behind. Chipmunks scattered out of my way. Scrambling in every direction, they darted under the cabin, into bushes, or up the trunks of the oaks.

Arriving, I spotted Michael staked out on a flat-topped boulder with a boy his age. Thank goodness. He had made a friend. Sandwiched between the girls was Mike. Holding song books, they sang along as staff plucked their guitar strings to "Mariah," my favorite camp song from *Paint Your Wagon*, by Frederick Lowe and Alan Learner. As a teen camper, my friends sang this song to me whenever they saw me. Back then, when we gathered, they broke into the chorus, *Mariah, Mariah, they call the wind Mariah.* This simple gesture always made me feel welcomed. Listening to my husband and kids as they sang the same song flooded me with contentment. I watched as my family effortlessly slid into the camp community.

The music swirled and I soaked in every detail. Observing my family as they relived the same experiences I had as a younger woman was fantastic. I hadn't realized how much I wanted my family to experience camp and moments like this, until right now. As Aretha Franklin said, "Music does a lot of things for a lot of people. It can take you right back, years ago, to the very moment certain things happened in your life. It is uplifting, it's encouraging, and it's strengthening." Our family had struggled in the past to slow down and make time for one another. But for now, we were united in song.

Practicing Gratitude by Singing Grace

The song ended, and staff set their guitars aside. Our kids followed the others' lead in returning their song books to the milk crate. Then they trailed them to the dinner bell, and everyone grabbed its rope. Tugging in unison so the clapper struck the bell, this was their first lesson at camp about working together. Ding! Dong! Ding! Dong! Supper was ready.

Staff served meals on a regular schedule: breakfast at nine, lunch at one, and dinner at six. The process was super-efficient. We gathered outside to prevent us from interfering with the workers. When our tables were set and waiting for us, we would enter and find our assigned seats. Eating family style meant the kitchen prepped the same food for sixty-plus families. Passing the platters around the table replicated how we ate at home. (Well, on those rare nights when we were all together.) Within minutes a peaceful dining room erupted into a cacophony of sound.

Michael and his new buds raced by me to hold open the doors. Entering, I noticed a quilt made of old camp t-shirts hanging on the stone wall. Mom had shared with me how a camper, Andrea, who I vacationed with years ago, had sewn this masterpiece. I'd have to remember to inspect it more closely at a quieter moment. Weaving through the dozens of round tables, I led Mike and the girls to ours. There were thirty in total and each one held two or three families. Recognizing our number, twenty-five, taped to the napkin holder, I stopped and stood behind my chair. Everything came back to me; the tradition was to sit after we sang grace. Standing allowed more room for others to walk through the dining hall. The same system of managed chaos still worked.

"Mom, what grace are we singing?" Mia asked. I

whispered in her ear, "The only one I recall is "Johnny Appleseed", and Grandma Jan always said it rained if we sang it."

Director Dave spoke into the microphone, "Welcome, grace will be 'Johnny Appleseed', the words are on the screen." Mia and I giggled.

> *Oh, the Lord is good to me*
> *And so, I thank the Lord*
> *For giving me the things, I need*
> *The sun and the rain and the apple seed*
> *The Lord is good to me, Amen.*

"Isn't this the grace your mom says brings a storm?" Mike asked.

"Yup, and she's never been wrong."

Nick Polizzi, director of The Sacred Science wrote in *The Art of Blessing Your Food* that saying grace had fallen out of fashion. "It was a ritual that had become less common in our busy modern lives. Family members snatched packaged food and gathered by the television or interacted with their devices instead of each other. Meanwhile, everyone longed for more connection to each other, to the earth, and to spirit."

Camp was in the business of building strong families and a binding community. One way was by expressing gratitude. I hoped our children learned the importance of practicing gratefulness. We had not been doing this at home. Going in different directions, we were guilty of being one of those families in Nick Polizzi's article. This pause before eating and taking a minute to recognize our blessings was a reminder. We had each other, food, and an hour to eat. Sometimes the songs were silly, which added to the enjoyment—we sang one of our graces to the theme of the TV show *The Adams Family*. It was not the words or the tune that mattered, it was the recognition we had much to be thankful for in our lives.

Pausing, I took the time to count mine. Mike wasn't in the World Trade Center collapse, and I had three children I loved to pieces. With the support of the camp community, I hoped to focus on meaningful values. I found myself smiling and laughing with joy. The week was off to a great start.

More on Communal Dining

A bonus of dining together was meeting another family right at the get-go. I could tell Michael was overjoyed when his new friend, Andy, was assigned to our table. Leaning in, shoulders shaking with laughter and participating with everyone, I knew he was happy. Andy, his sister, Kelsey, and their parents Doug and Jodi were a ton of fun. Within minutes it seemed we had known them for years. Sharing how they ran ragged all week and were grateful for this opportunity to reconnect created a common thread for us.

This conversation confirmed family mealtime was a habit I needed to work harder to maintain at home. With this first meal, I could already see the kids were engaged with one another. Instead of gulping their food so they could leave to do something else, they conversed. The ringing of the announcement bell interrupted my thoughts. Amazing how that sound quieted hundreds of people. The decibel level dropped, and Dave shared the evening's activities with us.

He recommended we head to the waterfront dock after dinner. But before we left the mess hall, the routine was for everyone to assist with cleaning.

"Mom, we have chores on our vacation?" Michael asked.

"Yup, it's part of the program."

"One I think is a good idea," Mike said to Michael while looking at me. At home, chores were a constant battle. And I was leery of pushing them as it was easier for me to do everything. Sigh, I knew enforcing them would teach the kids responsibility.

"Harumph," Michael said. Then he noticed his new friends were cooperating.

"Teamwork makes for dream work," Jodi said. Piling all the dishes together on one side of the table, our efforts saved time for staff. It amazed me to see our kids pitch in with a bit of encouragement. Deciding I would rededicate myself to assigning jobs at home, I needed to loosen expectations of having them done my way.

"Look, Mom," Michael said. "I stacked nine cups—this high."

"The napkins can be composted," Megan said.

When the work was completed, families headed out for the evening activities. There was fishing, boating, and of course the snack bar. Our kids raced off to get in line for the pontoon ride. Staying behind, Mike and I visited more with Doug and Jodi.

The guys decided to partner for the bocce ball tournament. Jodi and I planned a walk around the lake. When the dining hall emptied, we left to join the kids.

"We're too late," Doug said as our children scampered out of the pontoon.

"Oh no," I said. "I wanted to go with them."

"I think they had fun without us," Jodi said.

The kids playfully pushed and poked each other. I admired how they made friends with ease. With our recent move, my friend circle had become smaller. We were the family attending too many activities and then funerals every weekend. I cringed thinking of how my need for control almost kept us from coming on this last-minute trip. The night before our departure, I had panicked over the upcoming school year.

"I think we should cancel," I said.

"What? Why?" asked Mike.

"I have too much to do to get the kids ready for school."

"Like what? All they need to do is get on the bus."

"Well, I have to review their supply list, and make sure they have new clothes, and shoes."

"I'm sure they'll be fine with what they have."

"Yeah, but I want to prepare so they have a really good start."

"We should go. This is important."

"You know I'm not good at last minute stuff."

"I know, Hon. I know you love to have every detail nailed down. However, has anything changed since the 9/11 wake-up call and our need to focus on how fleeting life could be?"

"Nope, nothing," I conceded.

"Well then, let's focus on one another, worry about school later, and get our butts to family camp!"

"Okay." But it really wasn't okay. Doing something at the last minute went against my nature. Ugh, I realized how in my search for "the right way" to live I had created a comfort zone. I had needed his prompting to become flexible and open to what could be waiting for us at camp. Plus, I reminded myself, we already made new friends. And everyone knew friendships enhanced our lives. Having friends and spending time with them made us happier and healthier and got us living life to its fullest. This was a terrific beginning–for all of us!

S'mores

· · ·

After the pontoon boat emptied, Dave pointed to two staff members. They were pushing carts up the hill to the program lodge. The lodge consisted of the snack bar, craft shop, and patio.

"S'mores on the patio," he said.

When I was a teen camper, we waited for the last night for this treat. Finding the best roasting twig was a weeklong endeavor. We searched the ground while walking to our various activities hoping to find the ideal one. It had to be the right length, so you didn't have to stand too close to the flames and get smoke in your eyes. And a smooth one was best for sliding marshmallows on the end. You didn't want bits of bark in your dessert. Though I understood things evolved whether we wanted them to or not, I still thought the kids should have to wait, like I did.

"Let's go!" The kids pestered Mike and me as we approached them. Yanking on my arms, Mia and Megan pulled me up the hill. Michael, Andy, and Kelsey followed while chanting, *"S'mores, s'mores, s'mores."*

Dave lit the kindling and the wood started to burn. Gathering around the flames were a half dozen families.

"Who wants a s'more?" Mia asked.

Looking at each other, Michael and Mike shared a knowing smile. We had watched the movie *Sandlot* two nights earlier and, in the film, one of the neighborhood kids, Smalls, learned how to make one.

"What's a s'more?" Michael said, repeating Smalls' line in the movie.

"You're killin' me Smalls," Mike said. Then they quoted the scene line by line.

"First you take the graham," said Michael.

"You place the chocolate on the graham," Mike added.

"Then you roast the mallow."

"When the mallows are flaming, you put it on the chocolate."

"You cover it," Michael said. Then together they both said, "You stuff!" They imitated shoving a s'more into their mouths. It's a classic movie. Every family should watch it.

"I'm ready," Mia said. "Help me, Dad." She had a kebab skewer in her hand.

"Me too," said Megan. She pulled one out of the pile. Humph, they don't even have to look for a stick, I thought.

Mike kept an eye on the kids. And I kept one on him, hoping he toasted mine how I liked it, lightly browned on all sides making the inside gooey.

"Look, Mom, mine's on fire," Michael said. Waving it, specks of burnt marshmallow flicked off onto the ground. He laid the blistered mess on a graham. As he stuffed his into his mouth, the smoke shifted blowing into our faces.

"My eyes are burning," he said.

"Mine, too," said Mia. Rubbing them she hid behind

me. I gave her stick to Mike. Juggling ours, Mia's, and watching Megan made him parent of the year in my book.

Watching the kids licking their fingers, I waited. I willed him to turn and present me with ours.

"Look at these babies," Mike said. Finally, there were two caramelized beauties.

"Excellent," I said. I assembled the s'mores and held mine to my nose. Inhaling, I smelled smoke and vanilla. "Whoever came up with this combo was a genius."

"I want another," Michael said. Wiping his mouth, he smeared chocolate on his cheek.

"Me too, me too," said his sisters.

Mike looked at me with raised eyebrows. "Well, Mom, what do you think?" Wanting to limit their sugar consumption, I struggled to agree. Realizing special family time was difficult to find, I nodded. The kids high-fived one another and their enthusiasm made me glad I bent the rules.

"Yeah, I'm not burning mine this time," Michael said. He raced to the fire and put his stick right into the red-hot embers.

"Will you make mine?" Mia asked. "I want to sit with Mom." Tucking into my side, she plucked two chocolate squares off my lap.

"I'm good at this," said Megan. "I'll make my own."

I pulled Mia in to snuggle. I let go of seeking my vision of the ideal experience and how to manage the outcome. I embraced this occasion—by the looks of their sticky faces, my family looked like they had welcomed our first night with open arms.

Evening Walk

The fire fizzled and our first day was ending. We guided the kids to the cabin with the glow of our flashlights. Dancing the beams back and forth on the path, we concentrated on our footing. Mia was the first to hear the crunching in the tall grass.

"Let's go," she said. "I'm scared."

Grabbing my hand, she held firm. A light breeze rustled the leaves in the trees. She squeezed my hand tighter. Hoot! Hoot! We pointed our light in the direction of the call. We couldn't find the owl. However, our attention was drawn to the sky bursting with stars. Being so far away from urban lights made the heavens sparkle.

"There's the Big Dipper," Mike said.

Craning our necks back, we stood gaping at the sky's brilliance. Hundreds of stars twinkled at us.

"Look for a shooting star," I said. "Then you can make a wish."

"I think I see one," Megan said.

"Me too, I wish for another fun day," Mia had forgotten she was afraid. Reaching our cabin, the kids crawled into their sleeping bags and nodded off.

"A lot of stimulation," I said. "New friends, singing, and noshing on s'mores."

"And all this walking is sure to tire them," Mike said. I loved that they had worn themselves out after a day well spent. After turning their lamps off, we went to our side of the cabin. I realized I was flat out exhausted, too. Looking forward to joining the kids in slumber, I was surprised Mike didn't dim his light. Flipping open the activity sheet, he crinkled the papers. His finger hovered, and he said, "Hey, there's a guided birdwatch in the morning, nice!"

"Oh yeah, I forgot some campers share their expertise. When I was thirteen, a dad tried to teach me how to whittle," I said.

"How'd that go for you?" Mike asked.

"Whittle by whittle," I said.

"Boo." He whacked my arm. "Well, maybe you'll be better at bird sightings than jokes. Want to join me?"

"What time?"

"It starts at six a.m."

"Yeah . . . no, I'm sleeping in." I rolled over and snuggled under the fuzzy blanket. Before drifting off, I thought how our family was off to a good start of slowing and reconnecting. And, maybe, just maybe, I had enough courage to get cozy with the messiness of family life.

<h1 style="text-align:center">SUNDAY</h1>

The Bird Walk

Way too soon, Mike awoke and sprang out of bed. He laced his hiking boots, packed his camera, and bounded out the door toward his adventure at 5:45 a.m. I curled up for some more shut eye. An hour later, I woke to his voice. Wiggling to the edge of the mattress, I looked through the screen door and saw the kids gathered around him on the porch.

"Look at this critter."

Leaning in for a closer look, their gathered heads were picture perfect. Though I strained to hear the words he was saying, I heard the passion in his voice. Mike's enthusiasm was cute. Staying silent, as I didn't want to disturb this father moment, I moved near to listen.

"Whoa," Michael asked, "what is it?"

"It's a red-backed salamander. John, our guide, found it under a wet piece of cardboard," Mike said.

"Did you touch it?" Mia asked.

"Nope, if it's grabbed, it shakes off its tail."

"Aw."

"It's okay. John says they grow another one after they make their escape."

"Oh, it's tiny!" Megan said.

"When it uncurled, it was as big as your foot."

"Did you see anything else?" Michael asked.

"Yeah, John took us to a grove of cedars by the staff lodge."

"What was there?" Mia asked.

"As we approached, we heard a high-pitch whirring sound."

"What was it?" Mia asked.

"Cedar Waxwings," Mike said. "And guess what?"

"What?"

"Their wings look like they'd been dipped in lemon-yellow candle wax, like their name!"

It was terrific to see Mike's zeal. After one day of camp, he easily left "productive dad" at home. I saw a side of him I had missed. Inching closer, I leaned on the screen door to hear more.

"I thought we had seen everything, but John said we had one more stop," Mike said. "He took us to the horse barn."

"What was there?" Michael asked.

"Look at these." He showed the kids images of small plump birds with sea-blue heads and orange chests. "They're pretty rare. I feel fortunate to have seen one."

"It's pretty," Mia said.

"She's my favorite," Megan said.

The floorboard squeaked, and everyone turned towards me.

"Sounds like you had a momentous morning."

"It was incredible. I'm still giddy."

"This is a different Mike than I'm used to seeing," I said. "Normally, you're all business."

"I was a complete nature-goober."

I realized I didn't know everything about Mike. After fifteen years of marriage, he surprised me. He woke early to participate in an activity I had no inkling interested him. We had scheduled every moment of our lives to the point where we didn't leave time to explore. Sharing his joy with the children melted my heart, and I fell in love, again.

Town Hall

A camp-wide assembly, Town Hall, was scheduled after breakfast. We gathered around the fire circle, and the staff stood on the stage. The families then settled onto benches facing the stage and the 125-acre lake. The lake was the focal point of camp. There were water activities throughout the day and opportunities to view it from everywhere. I couldn't wait to run around it like I did as a teen. But first, Dave needed to officially welcome us.

He started a "repeat-after-me" song. Staff owned the verse and soon, everyone joined in. "There was a moose, who liked to drink a lot of juice." When the song ended, Dave provided a brief history of camp origins. The property started as a farm, transitioned to a health retreat, and finally found success when families started to attend during the summer of 1957. Today, the decades of commitment and work of others have led to a thriving family camp.

The families in attendance hoped to create a safe environment where everyone could flourish. This was the community my parents reminded me would help us. I didn't have to do it by reading a gazillion books.

Dave asked us to welcome new families to this tradition. He called out for first timers to stand. We clapped and cheered for all of us first-years. Moving on, he welcomed second year and so forth. A family of twelve stood when he hollered out, "Thirty-plus years." I counted three generations. Receiving a standing ovation, the grandparents beamed. I thought: What a gift to have sustained this tradition for so long.

"Mike, my parents started this for me and my siblings."

"Yup, and so far, it's looking like a good one for us to continue."

Next, staff introductions began. We learned which

counselors were to supervise our children. Besides the kids' leaders, we met waterfront, craft, nature, and kitchen employees. Finally, Dave introduced the small cohort of international students. I was thrilled to see this practice had continued. While two or three had traveled from the United Kingdom, others came from Eastern Europe, the Middle East, Australia, and New Zealand. This effort to bring young adults from around the world added a wonderful cultural flavor.

"Hey," I whispered to Mike. "My sister, Laura, was on camp staff for a few years."

"Really, I don't think I knew that."

"Yup, she was waterfront and program staff."

"Did she enjoy it?"

"Yeah, I was a little jealous that she got hired and I didn't."

"Hmm, well maybe coming back now will make up for that."

She had volunteered during high school while I was occupied with the swim team. Camp had a fabulous program to teach leadership skills, so when these young adults were in college, they were ready for staff. It was a fantastic way for young adults to give back to this community. I hoped our children would want to be part of this legacy of volunteers and staff. Then I could live vicariously through them.

Ending Town Hall, Dave asked us to introduce our children to their counselors. There were daily activities planned for them, such as canoe swamping, a hike to the spring, and tie dying. I was eager for them to join their groups. Not only for their own fun, but so I could have child-free moments, too. However, this morning, Mia clung to my legs, and Megan hid behind my back.

"I don't feel like going," Mia said.

"Me neither," Megan said.

I was surprised as their two new friends, Rachel and Becca, were there.

"Why not?" I asked.

"We don't want to do what they're doing!" Mia said.

"Why not?"

"It's a graveyard hike," Megan said. "Too scary."

"Oh, let's check with your counselor."

I walked with them to Nick, and he assured them the hike was fun. He introduced them to the other kids, and they widened the circle to make space for them. Turning away, I caught sight of a woman with pink streaked hair coming toward me. My turn for a little bit of fun.

Fast Friends

Tracy wore a pink skirt complementing the color of her highlights. Arriving at breakfast in my Reebok's signaled I was a fellow runner. Introducing herself, she asked if I'd join her in a loop around the lake. I accepted her offer. Recollecting how easy it was to make friends here as a youngster, I hoped to do the same as an adult. Charlie, Tracy's husband, and Mike had met each other at the sign-up sheet for the ping-pong tournament. Deciding to practice, they went to find paddles. I bounced with anticipation—a run and the potential for another new friend, how much better could it get?

Tucking her hair under a headband, Tracy said, "Thanks for running with me."

"I haven't had a running buddy for a while. This will be nice." I started to think how with each move I became a little more protective of my time. I had neglected to seek running friends. Tracy making the first move made me realize I needed to reach out to others as well. Sometimes it was easier to run alone and check it off my list. With a little bit of effort, I bet I could create a running community at home.

Starting on the road, we passed by the beach. We watched the lifeguards launch four women on paddle boards. Their laughter drifted to us.

"Cool," Tracy said. "I've always wanted to try."

We observed as the women tentatively stood from a kneeling position. Wobbling on the boards, they balanced themselves, and then started to glide. They cheered for each other and listening to them urged me to give it a go. Why not? I had read recently, as I scrolled through HuffPost, that adults forget how to make friends. Remembering one of the tips from the article on how to make friends, I tried one. I suggested we reserve a few paddle boards and learn together.

"We could try tomorrow," I proposed.

"Let's do it!" Tracy said, "I'm game." The advice worked and we had a date.

Settling into an even pace, we jogged up a hill through the trees and then back toward the lake. We weren't speaking as we trotted across the old, covered bridge. Clunk, clunk, clunk, our feet sounded funny on the worn planks. Tromping even louder for effect, I exaggerated my movements. Swinging my arms for leverage, I launched myself in a jump and landed with a thud. Tracy laughed and it felt good that she appreciated my goofiness.

We burst out from the cover of the bridge and onto the grassy landing of the earthen dam, I remembered it was the only flat part of this run.

"Let's go faster," I said.

Kicking into a sprint we raced the horse worn path. My previous experiences running with someone new were always a bit awkward—bumping elbows as each person tried to figure out body spacing. With Tracy it was seamless. Reentering the tree-covered trail, we slowed our tempo to navigate the uphill at the same time.

"Our paces match," I said.

"I'm really enjoying myself."

"I run most mornings."

"I'd love to join you," Tracy glanced at me.

"Perfect," I said.

"At home, I have limited time for friends," she said.

"Me, too! But that is because I keep my family too busy."

We opened to one another about our struggles balancing life. Sharing how hard we were on ourselves and how it trickled into our family relationships helped us to bond. A teacher, Tracy was aware of the over-scheduled family trap. It was unlike me to share my struggles with anyone. It was such a relief to talk with her. Choosing to be vulnerable with her was the moment we transitioned from strangers to friends.

Time flew by and we exited the woods by the horse barn.

"Hey, Mike saw bluebirds here this morning," I said.

"Want to look for them?"

"Nah, that's his thing," I said. "He's having a different experience than I did when I was a teen camper."

"Oh, you camped here growing up?"

"Yup, I forgot how much I loved it."

"Is it different coming back as a parent?"

"Yes, I'm constantly comparing."

"What do you mean?" Tracy asked.

"I want everything to be the same."

"Ah, the desire to share your life experiences with your kids," she said.

"Yeah, you nailed it."

"Well, maybe this week will be close enough?"

"You're right. So far so good."

"I agree, as a newbie I can already see the appeal of camp. My kids were welcomed right away."

Tracy already appreciated the community of belonging. Who cared if things were a little different? We had all made new friends, added grace to our meals, and relaxed into one another's company. The magic was in these simple moments.

Exiting a grassy meadow, we traversed an old aluminum dock providing our path over a bog. Covered in goose poop, it was slick. Slipping on a little bit of the droppings, I focused on my footing. A fat raindrop smacked me on my forehead breaking my concentration. Then another—the sky opened, and a deluge poured down.

"Let's race to those trees," I said.

The rain added to the slickness. Sliding, we hooted with glee. We clung onto one another to help us keep our balance. Reaching the pines and maples, we found respite under their massive canopy. Feeling the cold on my arms as the temperature dropped, smelling the wet moss, and hearing the fat raindrops splashing on the lake made me feel alive. This nature run was fuel for my soul. Instead of planning my day or repeating my mantra of "one day at a time," I fell in love with running again.

"We look silly," Tracy said.

"Ridiculous," I agreed.

Minutes later, we started again when the cloudburst turned to a drizzle. Leaving the shelter of the trees, we popped onto the main road. When we reached the office porch, we tucked in under the eaves. Shivering, we looked longingly through the window at the office staff with their steaming coffee mugs.

"I'm drenched. Hot cocoa?" Tracy asked. Going in looked inviting. What could be better than sipping a hot beverage after a cold rainy run? However, I wanted to go again.

"Nah!" I grinned, "Let's do another loop."

"Okay."

Our shoes squeaked as we stepped off the stairs. Sloshing in the puddles at our feet, we chuckled as dirt splashed on our calves. The clouds opened and another downpour started, this time with a blustery wind.

"Bring it on," I yelled. I shook my fist at the heavens. Adding to my wet dog appearance, I now had fogged glasses, and my shoes were saturated. I didn't care as I was having the time of my life. Tracy and I had been authentic with one another. She didn't care that I was silly or had parenting struggles. Our vulnerability in accepting ourselves as we were–was freeing. I ran like I felt, uninhibited, this time around even more enjoyable.

Shower House

Skipping to the cabin after our second loop, I grinned. I grabbed my shower cubby and bounced to the bath house. Peeling off my outfit, I stood under the cascade of the shower head and luxuriated in the heat. Already thinking of our next run, I appreciated the special bond Tracy and I had already created. She listened to me, and I felt heard.

Splashing and sliding reminded me of what it was like as a kid. Living in the moment. I remembered I used to judge how much fun a kid had based on how dirty they were by day's end. Watching the muck rinse off my legs, I realized I had exceeded my own standard.

Warming in the shower, I was rejuvenated. For women, pleasure can get lost in the transition to parenthood. At least it did for me. I took my role so seriously I often forgot to relax. Becoming so task oriented around baths, meals, homework, and other daily chores, I forgot to pause and be present. Making a new friend and relearning how to let go of expectations and play was one of the best parts of camp, so far. I didn't time myself. I didn't repeat my mantra. I enjoyed our time and ran purely for fun. (With a side of girl-friend therapy!) I couldn't wait to see what the rest of the day, let alone the week, had to offer. I bounded down the hill with a renewed sense of energy and youthfulness.

Men's Softball

Leaving my wet things to dry on our indoor clothesline, I walked to the sing-along area. The pattering rain drove the families inside. Everyone squeezed in near the fireplace built in a thirty-foot-high stone wall. Taking time to inspect the quilt that hung on the wall above the fireplace, I recognized t-shirts from years ago. Here was another example of how a long-time camper gave back to camp, like the bird-watcher.

Everyone was singing "We're going to Kentucky," so I joined in. *Shake it baby, shake it, and shake it all you can.* We were on the final chorus when staff signaled for the bell to be rung. The kids raced to return their song-books, ran outside to the entrance, and grabbed hold of the bell rope.

Arriving at the table alongside Mia, she reminded us that when we sang the *Johnny Appleseed* grace, it had poured like Grandma predicted. Tonight's song, "'Neath These Tall Green Trees," was a better choice.

Once we were seated, I described my run with Tracy. Everyone laughed at my reenactment of slipping and sliding on the poopy walkway. Poop is always funny to kids (and some adults).

"We went to the archery range," Megan said, "I got a bull's eye on my first try."

"When it started to rain, we ran to the bouldering room," Mia said.

"What is bouldering?" Michael asked.

"It's rock climbing but lower to the ground."

"If you slip, you let go," Megan added.

"And land softly," Mia said. "On the mats."

"Sweet. I hope my group goes," Michael said.

I was thrilled we were dining together. Instead of Mike coming home to leftovers and me filling him in on our day, he heard everyone's updates firsthand. The kids listened to one another. Mike caught my eye and winked.

"What does everyone want to do tonight?" I asked. I hoped to continue this sharing time into the evening.

"I'm playing softball," Mike said. "Campers vs. Staff."

"My guys and I are going," said Michael. "We volunteered to shag balls in the outfield."

"Girls, shall we go and cheer on Dad?" I asked.

"Can we get milkshakes after?" Megan asked.

"Yup, sounds good." Dave had announced the tubs of ice cream had arrived from the local dairy. "Let's help the staff first."

In addition to stacking plates and separating the compost, we placed the silverware into the "jig a lotta's" —containers so named for the jingling and tinkling sound the utensils made as they were transported to the dishwashing unit. Learning some of the staff were teen volunteers, our children were motivated to assist minus any fuss. After one day, they looked up to them, modeling their behavior. Stacking the last plate, I said we were ready to join the crowd. As we headed to the field above the parking lot, everyone chanted, "Here we go campers, here we go."

The girls and I held hands, skipped across the lot, and headed up a long flight of stairs. We arrived at a muddy mess. The field looked unplayable. Dave arrived with bags of sand for us to rake over the holes. After we completed that task, we wiped the bleachers dry for our bottoms.

"Wasn't it nice how everyone pitched in?" I said.

"Ba-dum-bump. Nice pun. I'm Sara."

"I'm Maria. There's my husband at bat."

"There's mine, stretching; he hasn't played since last year."

"If I remember, this is when middle-aged men act like they're in high school and someone gets hurt."

"Yup, last summer my husband's knee took a fast-ball. I teased him that we were going to have to take him behind the barn and put him down, like a lame horse."

Her sense of humor amused me! I chatted with her to see what other hilarious observations she shared, while our daughters made daisy flower chains. Meanwhile, Michael and his pals stayed deep in the outfield on the edge of the woods. They wanted to stop any balls before they got lost in the undergrowth. The dads were losing, but they didn't get discouraged. They kept swinging and started to put points on the scoreboard.

"It's getting close," said Mia.

"This was a highlight for Grandpa," I said. "He pitched and was always good for at least one hit."

"What else did Grandpa like to do?" Mia asked.

"He liked to play volleyball and cards," I said.

"And Grandma?" Megan asked.

"She took walks, knitted, and played cards with Grandpa," I said.

I enjoyed sharing what my parents did when they vacationed at camp in their younger years. In the future, when their grandpa told his softball team's story, this field would come to the kids' minds. Walks around the lake may remind them of their grandma picking through the wild berry bushes.

"You'll have lots to tell Grandma and Grandpa," I said, "when we get home."

"We just got here," Mia said.

"Yeah," Megan said. "Don't start talking about leaving."

They reminded me of my best friend, Jenni. My family brought her camping with us every year. When our car turned into the entrance, I had declared the week was already going by too fast. Jenni reprimanded me for mentioning the end before we even started. Megan and Mia's similar comment made me feel good. Confirming for me the decision to extend summer vacation was a good one.

Megan poked me in the arm. "Mom, it's tied."

It was the bottom of the final inning, and it was the staff's turn to bat. They had one out and a player on third base. The batter needed a hit for the go ahead run. Cracking the ball along the first base line, the dad playing first hustled to grab it. Tagging the bag, he made the second out. The third base runner tried to make it home for the win. The ball arched in over his head into the catcher's mitt.

The umpire called, "You're out, and we end in a tie!" The campers joined the catcher for a celebration dance. Everyone packed the equipment for the next week's competition.

"There's an ice machine," Dave said. "For any injuries."

Joining us, Mike said, "What a blast." Hobbling beside us, he winced as the girls hugged his legs.

"Are you hurt?" I asked.

"Nah, a little sore in the quads, but totally worth it, since I threw out a few base runners," he bragged. I knew what he meant; I loved the feeling of being sore from running. Like I had done my best and left everything on the trail.

We joined the other families heading to the snack bar. With good nature, everyone teased each other.

"Hey, Dave, next time drop the bat after a hit before you start running."

"At least I got one."

I knew the camaraderie of getting everyone together for a night of fun would last all week. Each event would build our connections over the coming days. Camp knew what they were doing in their efforts to support families. I looked forward to making more bonds over a milkshake. (I wasn't following my own sugar "rules" anymore!).

. . .

<u>We Gather</u>

Arriving at the patio, we saw foursomes playing euchre (pronounced you-ker), a mid-western card game. Also, a lengthy line of ice cream lovers snaked through the snack bar and out the doors. Michael and his pals were playing a rowdy card game in the corner. I knowingly smiled as my friends used to stake a claim on the same table each night. Suggesting we visit the craft room while we waited for the line to shorten, Mike led us to the stairs.

Reaching the second floor, we walked through rows of painting tables to the bisque ware room. Various ceramics lined the shelves. The girls picked gnomes to paint and fire in the kiln. Mike chose a serving bowl.

"I'm making this for my mom," he said. Turning the piece in his hands, he inspected it. His mother was an interior designer and appreciated a functional piece of art. I knew she would enjoy the bowl. I imagined it displayed in her armoire of collectibles. Thinking how sweet he was, at forty, to make something for her, I made a mental note to share this scene with her later.

We selected an available workspace and gathered our supplies. I assisted the girls with the cleaning of their pieces. Once everyone started to choose paint colors, I searched the ceramic aisle for inspiration. Not feeling creative, I went to the vision wall—an area covered in photos of past creations—to copy someone's craft. A picture of a colorful platter with thumbprints circling the sides jumped at me. Each one was underscored with the name of a family member. The focal point was the year the piece had been made. This would be an excellent reminder of our trip here when we used it at home.

As I chose five assorted colors, voices behind me reached a crescendo. Lifting my head, I scanned the room. The joy of community was in full swing: teens, singing along to the radio, were all folded in together on the sofas; staff guided some campers on the pottery wheels; and dozens of parents assisted little ones with their painting. An ache in my heart swelled with the realization of how much I had missed this place.

Catching my eye, Mike smiled and gave me two thumbs up. He and I had spoken of our other trips. While we had lots of fun in our summer travels, we suspected being in the mountains with this nurturing community would be more meaningful. The kids had the chance to create friendships and stories to last a lifetime. We should all thrive.

I rejoined my family at the craft table and shared with them my vision for the platter. I told them how this plate would create a memorable snapshot in time. They let me know which color they wanted their thumbs to be coated in. While I was organizing the paints, Michael bounded into the room.

"Mom, Dad, may I have money for a milkshake?"

"Let's all get one," I said. When I was young, my

father would give us money to use each day for a treat. When I asked him to spot me for the entire week, he refused. His reasoning was if I had to request money for each shake, it guaranteed he would see me occasionally. Aside from meals and a few organized activities, we all ran in different directions. I planned to use the same reasoning with our kids if the need arose.

"Dave said there are sixteen flavors," Mike said.

"I hope there are lots of chocolate options," Megan said.

"I'm going to try them all," Mia said.

We washed our brushes and laid them to dry. We planned to work on these pieces a little bit each day. Taking the stairs, we joined the shortened line. I watched staff scoop generous heaps of ice cream into the tall stainless-steel cups and add a little milk. While we inched closer, the kids changed their minds as they passed each flavor.

When it was Michael's turn, he blurted, "Moose Tracks!" Megan copied her big brother and then Mia followed along. The girls imitated him often.

"Might as well join the crowd," Mike said. "It has chocolate fudge, vanilla, and candy, yum."

"Not me," I said. "I'll have my favorite food. There's one with peanut butter."

We took our shakes and sat at an open spot. Straight out of the 50s, the tables were topped with Formica and trimmed with chrome. Sitting on the gray vinyl-covered chair, I reminisced.

"These are the same," I said. Running my fingers along the shiny chrome edges, I looked around to see what else was the same. I recognized the red stools at the counter, the vintage popcorn machine, and the chrome napkin dispensers. I imagined my friend Jenni and I walking in the door. As if I summoned her, she appeared, spotted us, and weaved her way through the other tables to join us.

"Auntie," the kids called. When I was six, my family moved into the house next to hers and we became attached at the hip. My parents invited her to join us each summer at camp after our first exploratory year. One doesn't have many lifelong friends, and I was fortunate to call her mine. And she was extremely lucky to get in off the waitlist right after us.

"Where is the rest of your gang?" I asked. Giving her an extra squeeze because hugs from someone you love are the best.

"They're in bed."

"Bummer, they're missing their first shakes," I said.

"Let me guess, something with peanut butter?" she asked.

"It's called Peanut Butter Revelry."

"Remember when I put a fake eyeball in your shake, and you were grossed out?"

"You were always playing pranks!"

"We were always pranking each other," she said. "In fact, I think you've been up to some trickery yourself."

"I'm not sure what you mean?" I gave her the side eye.

"Right after I let you know we were coming, we received a letter from the 'director.'" She made air quotes.

"You're so lucky," Mike said. Winking, he exaggerated it with a wide-open mouth.

"What did it say?" Michael asked.

"First years are required to perform a skit for campfire night."

"Oh, like an initiation for newbies?" he asked.

"Exactly," I said.

"Mom, do we have one?" Mia asked.

"Ah ha, the flaw in your evil scheme." Jenni wagged her finger in my face. "You have to let your family members in on the game."

"Ahem, we did receive a letter. I was saving it as a surprise," I said. "We're going to practice tomorrow."

"We have a skit?" Megan asked.

"There is no initiation," Jenni said. "I already asked in the office. They let me know I was being punked."

"Drats," I said. "Did you at least fake it to Scott and the kids?"

"I couldn't read it with a straight face." Turning to Mike, she added, "Maria printed it on *official* camp stationery."

"You did?" he asked.

"Well, I copied the logo onto résumé paper," I said.

"Pretty good, Mom," Michael said.

"I'm sure Jenni has thought of a way to get me back."

"Maybe."

The flickering lights signaled the snack bar was closing. Dropping Jenni off at her cabin on our way to bed, we revisited our first full day of camp.

"What was everyone's favorite part of the day?" Mike asked.

"My hike behind the office," said Michael. "There's a creek back there."

"Making a bull's-eye at the archery field," said Megan. "On my first try!"

"Painting my gnome," said Mia. "Did you know gnomes hide at the frog pond?"

"And you?" I asked my hubby.

"Too many to list. I've loved all of it," Mike said.

"Me too."

Arriving at the cabin, the kids tumbled into bed and fell instantly asleep, like the previous night.

"I changed my mind," I whispered. "This is my favorite part—the children snuggled in bed."

"I can't believe I've missed so many bedtimes over the years."

We watched them for a minute and then went to our side of the cabin.

"They are little angels when they're sleeping," Mike said. He kissed me goodnight. "Sweet dreams." Then he snagged the activity list and flipped the page to Monday.

I closed my eyes and reviewed the day. Making a

new friend, seeing an old buddy, and spending time with the family was great. So much better than falling asleep reviewing my to-do list and all the things I didn't get done. I dozed off thinking of a new way to punk Jenni. It needed to be safe and funny resulting in everyone laughing. Her cabin was visible for everyone to see on their way to the dining hall. Perhaps something that the entire camp could enjoy?

MONDAY

Couple Time

On Monday, all the programs launched. Tournament brackets were posted for all the various competitions. The kids had another activity, and there were many happenings across every corner of camp.

After dropping off the children for their supervised morning, Mike and I passed the bobbing sailboats and stopped at the kayaks. Choosing a double, we eased it off the dirt landing and onto the lake. Humming while he sculled, I saw Mike's shoulders relax.

"Is that a turtle?" I asked.

"I heard they are snappers," he said.

"One time I was swimming, and one went right by me."

"Anything else in this lake?" Mike peered into the

water. His question reminded me of the Lady of the Lake, a camp folklore about a ghost. Supposedly, on the way to her wedding, the horses spooked, and her buggy overturned. She died on the side of the road. There were many campers and staffers who insisted they had seen her in the past. They said she was a good spirit and had assisted them when they needed help. Like when the horses were agitated during a storm and ran away, she was seen calmly standing next to them until they were found. Only when all the horses were safely back in the barn did her apparition disappear.

Rocking, I banged on the bottom of the kayak. Grabbing the sides to steady himself, Mike glared at me.

"What? It's the Lady of the Lake," I said.

"Alright, knock it off," he said. "The Lady of the Lake, my butt."

As he turned to face forward, I wiggled the boat some more. He dipped his paddle into the water and splashed me.

"Ah!" I squealed. "It's freezing!" I threatened to soak him back. While I was tempted to escalate into a full-on water battle, I couldn't. We had drifted to the shore. It was too shallow to dig my oar in. In addition, there were a dozen or so fuzzy goslings with their parents. The adults charged us with outspread wings.

"Look at their black tongues," I said.

"They're hissing at us."

We heeded their warning and left them. The current

assisted us in our efforts by pushing us toward the middle of the lake. The rest of our time on the lake was a tranquil glide. We were quiet as we floated and basked in the warm sun. I didn't want this moment to end. Normally our time together was spent divvying-up action items and cross-referencing schedules. We had far too few snatched moments between tasks. Even that time focused on talking about the kids. I was so delighted to not have an agenda. This time together gave us the opportunity to do an activity we forgot we enjoyed and truly reconnect.

Three blasts from an air horn startled me. Triggering my memory, I explained to Mike what the sounds meant.

"That's the signal the waterfront is closing," I said. Heading towards shore, we entered the cove. Ross, a waterfront staff member, assisted us. Grabbing the boat handles, he guided us into an open slip.

"Thank you," I said. "We saw the baby geese!"

Mike said. "The closer we got the angrier the parents became."

"Yeah, sounds right," Ross said, chuckling. "One chased me twenty yards yesterday." Holding a hand for each of us to grab, he lifted us from the hull.

I thought of how the geese parents protected their babies. I was glad our children were safe in their age groups, so we were able to spend some quality time together.

. . .

<u>Crayfish</u>

"We should go check on the kiddos," Mike said.

After the morning activity concluded, kids reconnected with their parents at the sing-along area.

"I don't see them," I said.

"I'm sure they're okay; they'll turn up soon."

He began singing "Oh Stewball was a Racehorse" as he patted the space next to him.

"Sit."

Plopping my bottom beside him, I looked again. They were not at the bocce court, and they weren't waiting in line to ring the bell. I didn't see them anywhere. Ding, dong, the bell rang. By now, it seemed all the other parents had found their kids. A lump formed in my throat. I knew we dropped them off, but what happened to them? We agreed they were to meet us here. Where could they be?

"What do we do?" I asked.

Josh, Michael's counselor, walked by, "Hey Mr. and Mrs. Warner, I wanted to let you know Michael didn't join us this morning."

"Really?" Mike said.

Charlie and Tracy overheard, and Charlie said, "I just saw him in the bathroom."

"Thank goodness, I was starting to panic," I said.

"Did he tell you where he was?" Mike asked.

"Nope, but from the looks of his clothes, he had a blast."

"We need to find his sisters," I said.

"Oh, I saw them go into the women's bathroom," Tracy said.

"See, they are fine," Mike said. "Let's go in."

Josh held the door open for us, and we saw them standing at our table. I squeezed Michael's shoulder.

"Where have you been?" I asked.

His smile stretched wide. "We played in the creek behind the office. It was the best!"

His clothes were covered in dirt. Eyeing his sisters, I saw they were filthy, too. Megan had a twig stuck in her hair. Plucking the sprig, I inhaled the smell of creek water. Well, that and all the bug spray she wore.

"I had such a fun time, Mom," Megan said.

"Me, too," Mia added. "It was a blast."

I wondered why she was covered in more leaves than her siblings.

"I can't wait to hear what was better than being with your group," I said. All the other kids went to the activity, why did ours have to go it alone? As if Mike read my mind…

"Why'd you leave your counselors?"

"I promised the girls I'd show them the creek," Michael said.

"We didn't want to do what they were doing," Megan said.

"Why not? Group is where it's at," I said.

"We were playing dodgeball with each other," Mia said, "I don't like games where you have to run."

It's true, at her kindergarten assessment she refused to run. The gym teacher had asked her to jog between the cones. She put her hand on her hip, thumb in her mouth, and shook her head no. I was proud she had boundaries at such a young age. At the time, I had hoped she never lost the ability. Here she had an opportunity to test them again.

The kids started to tell us about their morning, and it was like watching a tennis match with all the back and forth.

Megan: Michael showed us how to catch crayfish.

Me: Crayfish, seriously? Don't they have pincers?

Michael, looking at his thumb and rubbing a red bump: If you don't catch them in the right spot, they get ya, but it only hurts for a second.

Megan: I caught the most!

Mia: Mom, Mom, Mom. Two boys helped us.

Michael: They saved bacon and dangled it off a branch.

Megan: Crayfish like the smell. They leave their hiding places for it.

Mia: If you get tired of waiting, you can lift the rock gently, so you don't scare them. Megan imitated slowly lifting a stone with her hands.

Megan: If you move it too quickly, then they dart away, FAST!

Michael: The water gets cloudy, and you can't see where they scurry to.

Mike: I used to catch crayfish when I was your age. There's nothing like an adventure mucking around and chasing those buggers!

Michael: We hopped on big stones to get to the other side.

Mia: I slipped and got stuck in the muck.

Megan: We linked hands to make a chain and pull her.

Mia, touching the scratch on her ankle: Look, my boo-boo doesn't even hurt.

Megan, touching each one as she counted: I have ten mosquito bites.

Me: What an adventure, group tomorrow, okay?

Michael: No way, I'm asking for extra bacon at breakfast.

Megan: I'm going back, too.

Mia: It's my turn to catch the most.

Mike: Some people called them "mountain lobster" when I was a kid. In parts of the country, people eat them.

I laughed knowing what was coming next.

Mike: Once Mom made a recipe with them, and it tasted like a dirty creek.

Mia: "Ew."

Megan: I just want to catch them.

Me: You didn't mind your sisters being with you?

Michael: Nah, they didn't bother me, like usual.

It made me happy he was looking out for them, and they were doing something together. I had been feeling bad because he spent all summer with his sisters. Here he was choosing to spend more time with them. It figured. My stomach had been tied in a knot worrying about something on their behalf, and they resolved their issue.

As they continued to describe each minute of their morning, my mind wandered to my explorations as a young girl. Jenni and I played in the woods behind our homes every chance we could. We'd build houses from massive branches and moss. Collecting feathers, bones, and rocks, we'd decorate our woodsy abode. We weren't supervised, yet we survived many scrapes. We were stung by yellow jackets and scratched from jaggers as hard as barbed wire. Glancing at my left arm, I rubbed the scar caused by an encounter with a hedge.

"I'm glad you're outside playing," I said. "And you stuck together."

"Are you suggesting it's okay if they skip?" Mike asked. He teased me because I never break the rules.

"Yes, please," the kids clamored.

"Well, I would prefer it if they went. That's what I did when I was their age," I said.

"They are making their own experiences," he said. "I think this day will live with them forever."

"As long as you tell us and your leaders, I don't see why not," I said

"I'm going to bring a bag to hold all the bacon,"

Michael said.

"I can't wait," Mia added.

Mike whispered, "Look how excited they are."

"I know. I have to remind myself they need to create their own camp history," I said.

Learning to let go was one of the reasons I wanted to return to camp so that the kids would have a chance to experience the power of making decisions on how to spend their days. So much of their lives was orchestrated; providing them a safe space to explore was empowering. I couldn't think of a better location than away from home, in the woods. One of the books on my nightstand was *Last Child in the Woods* by Richard Louv. He eloquently makes the point that being in nature reduces anger, fear, and stress and increases pleasant feelings. The author and my husband were right. Camp had started us on a new path. And our camp stories would become our favorite tales to tell. The adventures we created in the woods would remain in our hearts. After lunch we went to create more.

The Springs

That afternoon, Tracy and I relaxed on the beach while our kids played. Her two older girls were close to Michael's age. Her husband, Charlie, had decided to read on their cabin porch while their baby, Sage, slept.

Finding us after his horseback ride, Mike wanted to run with us to the springs. Michael assured us they would be on the playground for the afternoon, though I was leery to trust them after their disappearance in the morning. However, two generous parents offered to keep an eye on them. They reminded me how everyone at camp looks after one another.

So, we took off to complete the "springs challenge." This was an activity I never completed as a teen camper. Rain was the only reason I could think of that could have kept me from doing it. If I knew one thing, it had to be warm and sunny because the spring was chilly. I was excited. The kids weren't the only ones venturing into the woods. As our running pace and breathing settled, and we could speak, I confessed, "I've never completed this feat."

"Wait a sec, I let you talk me into doing something you've never done?" Tracy said.

"Uh ha. Yup."

"Okay, what did I get talked into?"

"First you jump into the really icy water and then swim to the other side."

"Easy peasy," Mike said.

"If the chilly water doesn't knock you for a loop, then you dive eighteen feet to the bottom."

"I can do it," Tracy said.

"There's one more thing…"

"Spit it out," Tracy said.

"You have to grab a handful of sand from the

churning spring hole."

"So…," Mike said.

"It's rumored if you get too near, you will get sucked in."

"I can't wait." Tracy pumped her fist in the air.

We reached the gravel road. Crossing the dam, we made a right instead of the left that Tracy and I had made the day before. Settling into an even pace, the quietness of the woods paled in comparison to yesterday's storm. The only sounds I heard were our feet on the path and our breathing. In the zone, we were completely self-absorbed.

Sinking further into the woods, we huffed it up the hill as the path narrowed. Shoosh! Shoosh! Shoosh! A small grayish-brown bird with a black-banded neck exploded from under a bush and landed at our feet. Appearing to have a fit, it flapped its wings and fanned its reddish tail feathers. Startling us, we stopped in our tracks as it stumbled away into the tall grass.

"What was that?" Tracy asked.

"It's a ruffed grouse!" Mike said.

"Did you see one yesterday on your bird walk?" I asked.

"No, but we had them in the woods behind my childhood home."

"Is it ok?" I asked.

"She's distracting us to protect her babies."

"Mission accomplished," Tracy said.

"Agreed," I said. "I don't want to mess with her."

"How lucky are we!" Mike exclaimed. "They're normally pretty elusive."

We watched for her reappearance.

"I think we're keeping her from returning to her nest," Tracy said.

"We should skip the spring challenge," I said.

"Why?" Mike asked.

"We'd have to come back this way again on our return," I said. "Wouldn't we upset her even more?" This was my chance to put the mother's needs before my desire.

"I agree," Tracy said.

Mike stood there dumbfounded, "Wait! What? You're giving up?"

"Yeah, we're mothers respecting another mother's boundaries," Tracy said.

Tracy and I looked at one another, fist bumped, and took off running. He couldn't argue with that. So, he joined us.

A mile later we ended our run at the dining hall. Adding our sighting to the nature board, I realized how amazed I was with each experience. One after another brought us full circle to our values. I had seen kindness in action, the practice of gratitude, sharing of chores, and now respecting boundaries. The spring would always be there, but the mother grouse needed us to show consideration for her babies. I walked out of the dining room knowing we had done the right thing.

. . .

Megan's Lesson

After our run, Mike and I returned to the children and the playground. Mia and Michael had created an obstacle course and were taking turns guiding kids through each challenge.

"That looks like fun," I said.

"It is," Michael said. "Did you do the springs challenge?"

"No, we were stopped by a grouse," Mike said.

"What's that?" Megan asked.

"A bird that flipped and flopped to distract us from her nest."

"How did that keep you from your swim?" Michael asked.

"Well, we respected her need to protect her babies, so we left her," I said. "By the way, where is Megan?"

They pointed to the program lodge patio.

"We're going to get a milkshake, want one?" I asked.

"As soon as we're done with our game," Michael said.

Stopping by the table on our way, Megan sat with four teenage boys. Stacks of poker chips hid her face.

"What's going on?" Mike asked. He dragged a patio chair next to Megan.

"Dad, you can't sit by me!"

"Why not?"

"This is a Texas Hold'em tournament. You can't help me."

"I didn't know you knew how to play poker," I said.

"These guys taught me." She motioned to the boys.

"Do you mind if we stay?" I asked.

"Nah, this is the last hand," one of the teens answered.

"Yeah, only because Megan is a ringer," another added.

"Awesome, Megs," Mike said.

"It's her turn to deal," another teen said. She shuffled the deck, allowing the kid on her right to cut it, and then dealt two cards to each person.

"How do you play?" I asked.

"This is called your *hole* cards," she explained. "We all take turns betting based on these." The kids all went around and threw a few chips into the middle pile. They used terms like *raise* and *fold*. There were four players left after this round.

"Now, I lay three cards, face up, which is called the *flop*," Megan said. "And we go again." Another player folded.

"Next is the *turn*," she said. She laid another card.

"And finally, the *river*." She flipped the final card. There were now two cards in her hand and three on the table. I thought these older kids must have been letting her win. I assumed they were showing classic family camp spirit. But I couldn't tell. They all had on their poker faces. One had dressed the part with a hat pulled over his forehead and another wore sunglasses, like you see on TV.

"Finally, we create the best hand between our two cards and the five communal cards," Megan said.

With her pair of fives and a five on the table she had three of a kind. One had a pair, and the other was bluffing. She won!

"I smoked you."

"You're a natural," the sunglass boy said. "Are you sure you have never played before?" He took off his shades and tucked them in his shirt pocket.

"Beginner's luck," Megan said.

They placed the chips and cards into the travel poker kit.

"I won a milkshake."

"We'll join you," I stated. Right on time, Mia and Michael joined us in line. As we ordered, the snack bar manager announced Megan's was on the house for being the champion. I swear she stood another inch taller.

"Weren't you intimidated playing with those older kids?" Mike asked.

"Nah, we had a few practice rounds."

"Did you have a strategy?" Mike asked.

"Well, I noticed those guys had habits."

"Like what?" I asked.

"Well, you know sunglass boy?" she asked. "He always touched them if he had a good hand."

"Good catch," Mike said. "Anyone else have a tell?"

"The boy on my left tapped his foot when he had a match."

"You should be proud of yourself," I said.

"Why? 'Cause I won?"

"Well, I was thinking because you were brave to join the older kids to learn a new game."

"Yeah, your mother and I are impressed."

Megan grinned, lowered her head, and slurped the rest of her ice cream. "I'm going to start playing at home, and I'll smoke you."

I pocketed this memory. Given the freedom to explore at camp she had discovered something new. Just like my recognition from Mike's bird walk. We left to change into something warmer for dinner. Listening to the kids buzz about her courage, I knew the camp values were soaking in.

Goofing at Dinner

After dinner, we waited for Dave to start announcements. When I was a teen, we used lulls like this for a little fun. I asked everyone at our table if they would join me in a "call out."

"What do you mean?" Mia asked.

"Well, one way is to pick on someone to stand on their chair and sing a song, like "I'm a Little Teapot."

"And the other way?" Mike asked.

"We can ask someone to skip around the room," I shared. "We sing 'skip around the room', and they can't stop skipping until we stop singing."

Our table decided on the second call out, counted 3-2-1, and we shouted in unison, "Hey Teens, skip around the room." Then all the campers joined in. We clapped hands and sang while every teen wove around the tables for a few rounds.

"That was fun," Megan said.

"I forgot to tell you something," I said.

"What?" Michael asked.

"Now, the teens will likely try and get revenge, by making us do something."

"Well, I know the words to "I'm a Little Teapot"," Mia said.

"Oh, do you?" Dave asked. He passed Mia on his way to the podium. Arriving at the microphone, he winked at Mia, "We have a request for a special song."

Mia buried her head in my side. "This is your fault, Mom. I don't want to sing in front of the whole camp."

"Well, since I started all this, we'll do it together," I said. I bit the inside of my cheek. I really didn't want to stand on my chair and sing either, but I got her into this mess. Mike adored attention. Maybe I could talk him into taking one for the team.

Dave began growling the lyrics in his deep voice. "I'm a little teapot short and stout . . ." Repeating each line after him, staff joined in, like a platoon. This was not the version we learned in pre-school. This adaptation was rowdy. Everyone caught on, started to clap, and repeated the lines. He slapped his legs in time with our clapping as he strode around the room. Ending right behind Mia's chair, he growled, "Just tip me over and pour me out!" (You can find videos of this version on YouTube.)

Everyone enjoyed the silliness and had fun. It was a simple way we created joy for one another. Glancing at Mia, her face beamed from the attention. Dave strode back to the podium. Providing the details for the evening activities, he asked us to carry our enthusiasm out of the dining room with us into International Night, which was the next organized event.

<u>International Night</u>

We walked next door to Alexander Hall, the old dining room turned into a multipurpose center. Tables had been set up along the walls, one for each represented country. Covering them were flags, books, food, and toys. The Internationals shared a little bit of their home with us. Tonight, we visited England, Mexico, and Estonia.

The International employees were dressed in the authentic clothing of their countries. We recognized the colorful skirt from Mexico and the English bowler hat. But the white linen top and full red skirt from

Estonia was new to us. We played trivia, sang songs, and ate their favorite foods. Mike asked them what their biggest surprise was coming to the U.S.

"Seeing the Statue of Liberty," Thomas said. His English accent made the girls giggle. One of their favorite cartoons was *The Wild Thornberrys*, a British family that documents nature around the world. Hearing his accent reminded them of Mia's habit of talking in her sleep using The Queen's English.

"I'm surprised there's dessert at every meal," Alma added. From Mexico, she noted her country's sweets were more subtle and not as sugary. For example, fruit with a kick of spice was served after a six-course meal. (As a side note, years ago the staff once gave us canned peaches after lunch and the whole room repeatedly chanted "Fruit is not dessert" for a minute. It was all in wholesome fun. But I digress.)

Sofia, from Estonia, said, "It's amazing how everyone in America is so nice. So, what do you kids like best about tonight's festivities?"

"The candy!"

I'm glad we supported these young adults. Sharing with one another helped us find our common ground. Mike learned of the Estonian's fondness for their rye bread like his family from Slovakia. Mia and Megan recognized the English "Ring around the Rosie" song. The flags impressed Michael. I appreciated the colorful clothes. In the matter of an hour, we celebrated our similarities and differences.

Being interested in the international staff's country and culture was another value that camp helped me recall. So much of our recent past had been spent trying to understand why terrorists had attacked us. This evening had brought me out of that mindset. Those young adults reminded us that most people had more in common than not. I hoped we continued learning and remember that they enriched our cultural understanding, expanded our community, and brought fresh perspectives.

We continued our conversation as we walked to the cabin for some snack bar money and flashlights.

"I learned the Internationals have a few weeks at the end of the summer to travel before heading home," I said.

"Don't they want to go straight back to their families?" Mia asked.

"Probably, but for most of them this is a long way, and they may not return for a while," Mike said. "If ever."

"Do you think they'll come to our house?" Michael asked.

"Maybe," I said. "Let's invite them."

"Hey, there's Aunt Jenni sitting on our porch," Mike said.

Note: We did have a few staff visit us in their travels. It was great to provide them some hospitality after they took care of us.

Prank Reprisal

"Oh, hi. I was in the laundry room. Decided to wait for you," Jenni said as we approached the porch.

"We need some money. We can all go to the snack bar together," I said.

"Excuse me," Mike said. "I have to hit the bathroom."

"I'll grab some cash," I called to him. "You kids want to head along? We'll be a minute."

Mike was back in a jiffy. "There's an 'out of order' sign on the toilet." I poked my head in the bathroom and read the note. We hadn't reported it was broken. It was odd for maintenance to come check on it.

"Oh, someone came by our cabin earlier and checked ours, too," Jenni said. "Everything was fine."

"The note says a plumber will be here in a few days," Mike said.

"Bummer, your toilet isn't working," Jenni said.

"Let's stop in the office and get the details," I said.

"I have to go, now!" Mike said. "I'll use the one in the bath house." He danced a little bit, like a kid who had waited too long and now it was an emergency.

Jenni and I were halfway to the office when she cleared her throat, "Ahem, don't go in and complain."

"Why not?"

"Didn't you recognize the handwriting?"

"It was you!" I shook my finger. "I should have known—all those letters we passed back and forth on the school bus."

"I didn't think you would go to the office. I looked forward to giggling every time you went to the bathhouse."

"Can you imagine their confusion if I went in there and demanded a working toilet."

"Yeah, that's why I had to stop you. It was worth it to see Mike race walk to the bathroom, though."

"Should we tell him?" I asked. "Or shall we keep it our secret?"

"I had enough fun at his expense," Jenni said. "C'mon, I'll help you remove the duct tape." We arrived back at the cabin at the same time as Mike. When I told him how we were duped, he gave her the hairy eye.

"I don't want to be on your bad side, buy you a milkshake?"

"Deal," Mike said. We linked arms and went to find the kids. I was quiet as they ribbed one another. Sizing Jenni up and down, I realized she fit right in at camp with her basic clothes. She had on black leggings and a grey sweatshirt. Would it be funny if I found a lot of colorful frilly clothing to hang from her outdoor laundry line? My wheels turned, where would I find some? Maybe the Internationals had some extra costumes they could share?

<u>Mia's Lesson</u>

Waking to the sound of the kids' squeaky screen door, I looked at my watch. It was only eight in the morning, and one of the kids was already awake. So far, they had been sleeping in until the first bell rang at 8:30 a.m. I didn't recall anyone telling me they had plans before breakfast. Peering into their side of the cabin, I looked to see whose bed was empty. Mia was gone. Where was she going?

I quickly slipped into my Teva sandals, headed out the door and followed her. I kept my distance to prevent her from hearing me so I could spy. Dawdling as she walked, she picked up a long branch. Trailing it behind her, she made a line in the dirt. Her dally turned into a skip. Boy did she take after her father, both waking in pleasant moods. Having strolled to the playground, she kicked her flip-flops off and jumped into the sand. Poking her branch in a hole, she patted a mound around it until it stood on its own like a flag. She filled a bucket with water. Then mixing it with sand, she dumped it and shaped a tower into place.

Hiding behind a big oak, I wondered if I should let her know I was there. Before I decided, a mother with her toddler arrived. I saw her speak to Mia, and it looked like introductions were being made. Mia tapped the spot next to her and handed the little boy the shovel. Plopping beside her, he started to scoop sand into the bucket. Leaving them to play, the mom moved to the side and opened a magazine. Mia and the child created another tower. A few more moms and tots joined the gang. So, this is what the mothers with young kids do before camp gets humming with breakfast and activities.

Smiling, I remembered all my mornings of shuffling our three kids to the local playground for some mommy time. It would have been easier to stay at home. However, my desire to connect with other moms was strong. I prepared the diaper bag, loaded them into their car seats, and drove to the park. If I missed going, I was off kilter. I needed their encouragement. Visiting with other mothers had faded in time as the children entered school. I yearned for those supportive conversations. We leaned on one another for advice. Some moms had older kids and I could learn from them, while others had little ones and I could be the expert. Who was I kidding? We were all doing the best we could with children that were all "unique."

Watching Mia include all the youngsters in the construction of a moat reminded me how cooperation was a lesson she had learned from the playground. There were always toys to share and turns to take. The park etiquette had sunk in. She led the kids one at a time to the lake to dip the bucket into the water. Carrying it together, they emptied it into the trench. Jumping into the moat, chubby toddler fingers and toes squiggled in the mush.

Normally, a child Mia's age didn't play with toddlers. At camp this was a daily occurrence. Kids of all ages played together often. Sometimes it was organized, like the afternoon canoe swamp between Michael's and the girls' groups. Other times it was more free-range. The ability for the kids to roam provided opportunities for creativity, curiosity, and confidence, not to mention mingling with kids of different ages.

I had rarely watched the kids play unnoticed. How often are we able to do that? I was so thrilled I had hidden from Mia; I could barely contain myself. I desired to say to the other mothers: Look how wonderful she is and how wonderful I must be to have raised her. Meanwhile, I knew she was a combination of all kinds of good influences. Neighbors, teachers, friends, and family—we all have a part in helping kids grow into decent humans. Now, I was reminded of how camp plays a part in this, too. Camp was more than another vacation. The values we wanted for our kids were being lived right in front of my eyes.

I stayed tucked behind the oak and watched. She was patient, making sure they each had a turn with the sand toys. I saw them all looking at her for social cues. Mia idolized the older kids when she was with them, but now she had the chance to be the leader. As I continued to surreptitiously observe this remarkable scene, one of the toddlers stood and stumbled. Knocking over one of the towers, he burst into tears. I inhaled sharply. Holding my breath, I waited to see how the other toddlers reacted. Mia quickly scooped him from the sand and dusted off his bottom.

Then she encouraged everyone to pretend they were giants stomping around flattening everything. I heard them squealing with pleasure. Knowing the accidental destruction of their castle could have resulted in tears, I was pleased at the turn of events. Mia handled the situation and turned it into something fun.

The sudden outburst of wholesome laughter drew the moms' attention. It was the best sound hearing all those kids giggling. The breakfast bell rang, and everyone started to gather their belongings. I called Mia. I wanted to catch her doing something good. I knew words of encouragement would be appreciated. It's too easy to point out all the things the kids needed to improve, at least it is for me: do a better job combing your hair, wipe the milk off your face, sit straighter, and so on.

"Hey honey, I've been watching you. You are really good with toddlers."

"You saw?" She slipped her hand into mine and beamed.

"The whole thing, I especially liked when you had everyone smash everything." I stomped my feet as if I were helping to demolish the spires.

"Well, remember when we were at the beach and Daddy's sand alligator got smooshed," she recalled. "He said, 'let's tromp it flat and start again, and make it better.'"

"Good advice, you set a really splendid example."

"I was afraid they would start to cry."

"Well, your quick thinking was awesome."

"Thanks, Mom." She squeezed my hand, let it go, and skipped ahead of me. What a morning. It started with me wondering where my daughter was headed to and ended with an experience I will remember for the rest of my life. She was an awesome little lady. When I tuck her in this evening, I will remind her of the good that she had done today. It made me want to bounce with joy. Joining her in three large hops, I snatched her hand back, and we skipped back to the cabin together.

Nature Stops the Game

. . .

After breakfast, Michael and the girls dashed away to their canoe swamp—capsizing and filling your boat with water. This was an activity they were excited for. At a designated signal all the kids would flip their boats and scramble to swap. The fun was seeing who ended up in which canoes and meeting someone new. Instead, I walked to the patio with my book, while Mike and Doug went to compete in the next game in their bocce ball bracket.

"Come watch volleyball at noon?" Mike asked. I nodded and caught Tracy on the path. She had a paperback as well, and it appeared we had the same idea of how to spend our late morning. Relaxing in the Adirondack chairs above the bocce courts, we talked. In the pauses of our conversation, I was drawn to the noise on the bocce court. Occasionally, I picked out Mike's voice. His volume matched the clanging balls that got rolled down the court. Being closest to the pallino, or smallest ball, earned you points. I could tell how the lead changed based on his silence or hoots. At the conclusion of his competition, he called me.

"C'mon, hon, I need your good karma. Last time you watched volleyball, we won."

Volleyball was one of the tournaments that attracted a lot of fans. If you weren't playing, you were probably scoping the competition. The two courts are next to the main trail through camp, nestled between the dining hall and program lodge. A lot of foot traffic passed by. No matter what you were doing, you saw and heard the games. Whistles blown by the referees, calls from team-mates for the next hit, or the balls being smacked by an open palm.

I packed up my bag and left Tracy to her reading. Settling in on a bench I watched the game, my head swiveling back and forth as the sides bumped the ball to one another. I cringed as I recalled why I had stopped playing the sport as a teen. In my last game, and the reason it was my final one, a ball hit me in the face, breaking my glasses into three pieces. That was when I realized I preferred sports where I was in control—like running and swimming. I preferred sports where a ball didn't travel AT me!

Scooching over on the bench, I made room for Scott, Jenni's husband. Her side was paired against Mike. Teasing one another, they stopped their warmups and took their positions. The tournament coordinator had named the squads after breakfast cere-als. Mikes was Cap'n Crunch and Jenni's was Count Chocula. Dressed like their team names and characters, a few competitors drew attention with their outfits.

"Looks like Halloween," I said.

"I saw them searching the wardrobe closet," Scott said.

"There's a wardrobe closet?" I asked.

"It's next to the boulder wall," he answered. "Filled with costumes."

"Oh, so you can find something for your campfire sketch?"

"Yeah," Scott said. "I'm dressing like the plumber who is fixing your toilet."

"Ew, good one. I guess it's my turn for the next prank."

"You know you can't beat her at this."

"She is crafty; she really got Mike with the broken commode."

"Speaking of Jenni and Mike, they have quite a volley going on."

The match had started, and the score was close. We were riveted as the lead changed depending on who had the serve. It came down to who made the most unforced errors. Mike's side won the first round and Jenni's the next. The tie breaker had started when a commotion drew our attention. Play stopped.

"Look!"

Circling high above us, a large bird pumped its wings in slow beats. Higher and higher it rose until it was a small speck. Then, swooping low, we easily identified an adult bald eagle. The striking white head was unmistakable. Murmurs of "It's an eagle" rippled through the crowd.

"It's the mother," the referee said. "She was around earlier with her young'un."

She danced, alternating between diving to the water and soaring to the clouds. Back and forth she narrowed her circle. Spreading her wings wide, she dove to the lake, and then suddenly stopped. It was as if she put the brakes on! Her stretched talons snatched a fish.

"Whoa!"

"Amazing," Scott said.

We tracked her flight as she flew into the pines.

"It's lunch time for her little one," Scott said. How satisfied the mother must feel to feed her child, I thought. Like when I take the time to plan healthy meals. Or when we cooked for neighbors.

"I've never had a game stop," the ref said. "So great." When he had everyone's attention back on the court, he blew his whistle to restart.

"Michael learned in his class the Native Americans consider bald eagles sacred," I told Scott.

"Why?"

"Because they fly high in the sky, near our Creator."

"How cool they're flying over our camp."

He turned back to the game. However, my eyes were continually drawn to the treetops. Wishing the mother would return to show off her magnificence, I tried to will her reappearance into existence. After a few moments, I realized I was being selfish, as if she were there for my pleasure. My junk value of arrogance had barged in. Thinking of Richard Rohr, priest and author, I recalled one of his pieces. He wrote how nature is a mirror of God. Seeing the mother eagle felt spiritual. In my mind, I compared the bald eagle's return to camp to my return.

Everyone in my clan was being cared for. Mike escaped the demands of life and had discovered his inner child while running from one interest to the next.

The kids were exploring the marvels of nature. I was moving into a more positive mindset, and I had also realized from Scott's tidbit about the wardrobe closet that I now knew where I may find some items to hang from Jenni's laundry line. My soul joined the eagle soaring in the sky. I looked forward to sharing my eagle analogy with Mike and the gang at lunch. (And raiding the wardrobe closet when no one was looking!)

Afternoon Fishing

Over chicken noodle soup and salads, I did just that. Michael said his leader, Josh, knew where the nest was, and they were going on a hike to see it in the morning.

"Even though it's high, it's large enough to see from the ground," he said.

"Watching the mother snatch a fish made me want to cast a line myself," Mike said. "Who wants to join me?"

"I do, me too, me three," the kids shouted.

"I'll watch," I said. Hooking worms made me squeamish.

"Let's get the gear Grandpa packed for us," Mike said. We gathered a digging tool to find worms, the rods, and a folding chair for me.

"I know an unspoiled spot." He guided us to a quiet nook.

The sun was tucked behind the hemlocks. Explaining to the kids how shade is where the fish hide, as if under a blanket, Mike set them up in their own spaces. Each one chose a pole and waited for him to set their hook. I sat behind everyone, so I wasn't being nicked by any wayward casts. Thinking of the realities of three kids trying to learn how to fish for the first time, I inched my seat back even further.

"Help me first," Mia asked.

"I'll be right there," Mike said. "Youngest first." He assisted Megan and then moved on to Mia.

By the time Mike reached Michael, Megan had tangled her line in the pussy willows. Leaving Michael, he hopped a few stones over to assist her. Looking to see if Mia was having any luck, and I noticed her pole laying on the ground. She was gathering a pile of rocks. Chucking a few into the water, she scattered the fish in every direction. She seemed unfazed by her actions. Meanwhile her brother looked at her in exasperation. I watched with wonder as Mike juggled his attention from one kid to the next.

Finally, he reached into the tackle box for bait to prepare his own fishing pole. Casting, he sailed his line and the bobber collided with a skipping stone.

"Did everybody see?" Mia shouted. "Three skips!"

Mike said, "Yup, me and the fish."

"I'm done anyway," Megan said.

"Me too," added Michael.

They set their poles next to my feet and raced away.

Skipping behind them, Mia joined them at the horseshoe pit. I turned back to Mike.

"Was that fun?" I figured he might be angry with them for quitting.

"Sure, small bites to keep them interested," he replied. He moved to a different position and continued casting his line. Leaning back in my chair, I caught all the sounds of nature. There were honking geese, leaves rustling, and water lapping. The kid's voices rose above the clanking of the horseshoes. I could hear them talking to their friends.

"Our dad took us fishing over there," Megan said.

"He didn't even get upset when I skipped a stone by his bobber," Mia said.

"Yup, he's the best," Michael said. While they described how their father tried to teach them how to fish, I realized it wasn't catching a fish that mattered, it was more important they spent time with their dad.

"Hey hon, I had one on the hook, but he got away."

"Oh well, you've accomplished something way better."

"What do you mean?"

"I'll tell you later," I said. "I'm eavesdropping on the kids." I used to measure success by money. Camp reminded me there were more important values. These few days taught me that a healthy family was what I should be working towards. I couldn't have been more pleased with how things were going.

After fishing, Mike reminded me it was time to

make our version of chili for the evening's chili cook-off. I liked to find recipes, shop for the ingredients, and prepare the food. As usual, though, I left the final cooking to Mike. Our different skill sets complemented each other. We had the perfect balance. I helped him carry the fishing gear to our room and found our secret ingredient—a dark chocolate bar.

Chili Cook-Off

"Is that enough chocolate?" Mike asked. "And where did you hide that?" He tried to find my secret spot to see if there was more.

"Our information packet said the servings would be in those little medicine cups," I said.

"Oh, good point, I guess there will be some other competitors, too."

Entering the industrial kitchen, the chef waved us over to our station. He brought us to a burner with a large pot. Standing on a stool to reach the top of the huge crock, I dumped the cans of beans and crushed tomatoes into the wide opening. Mike measured the spices and sprinkled them in. Swirling in the dark chocolate, our chili turned a rich caramel color.

"Yours looks awesome," Renee said. She grinned and mixed in a can of soda. "My mystery item."

"No way," I said. "Our kids won't believe you can put soda pop in chili."

"Mine is lime juice," said Jim. I had met them both in the art room.

"I hope you share your recipes," Mike said.

The chili simmered while we cleaned our spills. Chef offered to transfer the pots to the BBQ. We left, proud of our contribution to the evening's buffet. This simple activity created more bonds, we learned different ingredients to try, and we had fun. I looked forward to sampling and voting for the best one.

Working with those ingredients made me hungry. I was anxious to get our picnic blanket from the cabin and meet the kids for dinner.

<u>BBQ Picnic</u>

Our small cohort of cooks weren't the only ones assisting with the BBQ. Parents shucked corn, flipped burgers, and cut watermelon. The picnic area was a beehive of activity. Dinner was loaded on a hay wagon. An ingenious and unique way to feed all of us. Diners scattered at picnic tables, folding chairs, and on the grass. I felt like a cast member from *Sound of Music*—the scene where Maria and the kids hiked and picnicked. Lounging under the soaring oaks, it was as idyllic as one imagined.

After guiding the kids through the line and piling our plates, we found an open grassy area. Unfurling our blue and beige striped blanket, we settled in for our feast. Eating in the fresh air helped me to unwind after another pleasurable but jam-packed day. Why was it that everything tasted so much better eating al fresco? I leaned back on my elbows and took in the scene. The setting sun made the water sparkle, the grill smells wafted to us, and conversation buzzed. It was then I noticed the hot dog and chili station.

"We forgot…the chili!"

"C'mon kids," Mike said. "Let's go get some samples."

"I'm full," Mia said.

"I want another brownie," Megan said.

"There's chocolate in our chili recipe," I said.

"And soda pop in someone else's," Mike said.

"Pop! I'm trying that one," Michael said.

They ran off to try the samples and brought me one of each. They waited for me to taste them all before we voted. Mike had the voting slips and showed us how to make a little tear next to your favorite one.

"I like them all," said Michael. And he voted for them all, making a little rip for the five candidates.

"I'll vote for your chocolate one, but I'm still getting another brownie," Megan said.

"The pop one was fizzy." Mia smacked her lips. "It was my favorite."

"Ah, the results are mixed," Mike said. "I like ours the best."

"I like the one with limes. It tasted tangy," I said.

Mike took the slips to the voting jar. When he returned, he asked, "What's next?"

"Brownies!" Megan said. The kids raced to the hay wagon.

Mike said, "And you were worried if coming was the right decision."

"Now I'm wondering how we'll ever get them to leave."

"It's only Tuesday, don't be thinking about the end."

"I know, and there's so much more to do."

"Let's appreciate what is happening right now."

"Like another brownie?" I asked.

"Yup, let's go," he said. Offering his hand to help me from the blanket, he held it in his as we joined the kids. Besides trying the different chili recipes, I looked forward to the evening event–family games. Like a picnic, they reminded me that we didn't need to be entertained by Broadway shows all the time. We could create our own fun: hosting a chili cook-off at home, old-fashioned amusements, or inviting neighbors over for dessert. Choosing our brownies, we ate them on the way to join our team.

<u>Family Games</u>

·   ·   ·

Our pre-arrival checklist had us assigned to Team Orange, so we spotted them easily. Donning the orange t-shirts, we dug deep out of our closets at home before we came, we joined the others. Around the field, the rainbow was equally represented with teams of all colors. The kaleidoscope of families waited for instructions.

Kevin, our leader, was dressed in various shades from his head to his toes: an apricot hat, melon t-shirt, pumpkin basketball shorts, and papaya high tops. As a solo athlete, it had been a while since I was part of a squad. I was anxious as I wasn't used to playing with others. But not the rest of my gang. Mike oozed with eagerness, and the kids wiggled with excitement.

"Head to the beach," said Kevin. "And on our way, start thinking of a cheer." Following our leader, we prompted our kids for their knowledge of chants. Someone had to have sung a song in school or scouts, right? Renee and her daughter, Emma, started singing a little ditty. We quickly agreed on it as our anthem.

"Ok, what do you have for me?" Kevin asked.

We started singing. The tune was a kindergarten song that sounded familiar, and everyone chimed in.

O-R-A-N-G-E

Orange is what that spells.
Jack-o-lanterns are always orange.
Carrots are also orange.

Oranges are always orange.
O-R-A-N-G-E

. . .

"Nice, good for our first points."

"What's the next challenge?" Renee asked.

"Fill-the-bucket!" Kevin demonstrated how to play the game, and we arranged ourselves in a water brigade.

As I waited my turn, I stepped aside to see how the kids were doing.

"I didn't lose a single drop," Mia said. Giving her two thumbs up, I thought how wonderful that this game included all ages. It was another way staff worked hard to involve everyone. I also met a whole bunch of campers, which was another benefit. I knew from previous years that we would continue to recognize our team membership when we crossed paths during the week. Solidarity for orange!

While I mused, I passed two cups of water down the line until Kevin called, "The bucket is full." He checked our completion on his clipboard and congratulated us. "You all get extra points for full cooperation, too."

Walking us to the next station, it was time for the classic three-legged race. The kids started to organize themselves by size, so their strides were similar.

"Look at all these kids taking charge," I said.

"Outstanding," Mike agreed.

Tripping on each other's feet, they giggled all the way to the finish line. Our tally grew as the number of pairings crossed the finish. Forgetting us, our kids raced off to the next event. Ending with a pie toss and balloon stomp, we gathered on the patio to total the teams' points.

Green had the highest score. Dave announced they could redeem their prize at the time of their choosing.

"Drats, we didn't win," Michael said.

"I wanted the prize," Mia added.

"What is it, anyway?" Megan asked.

"I know what it is…," I said. "And I think you'll be glad that our team lost."

"Well, don't keep us in suspense," Mike said.

"I'm pretty sure it means he gets pushed in the lake by Team Green," I said.

"But the water is cold," Megan said.

"Yup, and he'll probably drag a few of the green team members in with him," I said.

"Sounds like a victory for everyone," Mike said. "We all get to cheer and laugh while Dave takes a chilly plunge."

"Let's go ask the green team when they plan on throwing him in, so we can watch," I said.

We strolled over to congratulate them and get the details before we headed to the cabin for the evening.

WEDNESDAY

<u>Morning Watch</u>

While most of my days began with jogging, Mike attended "Morning Watch"— an informal spiritual program. This morning, he asked me to join him. He shared how each session started with a short video focusing on a topic and then Dave opened with a question. Yesterday's subject was forgiveness. Mike said listening to the others helped him realize he wasn't alone in his experiences.

"The other parents shared how lonely parenting can be," he said.

"Sounds like kvetching," I said.

"Nah, it's more around not being so self-critical. Recognizing we all make mistakes."

Wow, that did sound like me. I wasn't enjoying

being a parent in our hyped-up, overscheduled world. Perhaps there was something to this. We entered the game room side of the snack bar. Tables with board games and puzzles were cleared and the chairs turned to create a semicircle. I greeted a few of the folks I knew. There were twenty adults. Jenni sat on my right, and I couldn't help but notice her left hand was tucked into a sock.

"I forgot my hand puppet," I said. "Is this a secret initiation?"

"Want some?" She pulled her hand out with a fistful of walnuts. "I brought a little snack."

"Nah, gray squirrel, gray squirrel, swish your bushy tail," I sang.

At least being with Mike and her was comfortable. Still, my stomach was a little ill at ease. I envied people of strong faith who spoke firmly of their beliefs. I had been a seeker my entire life and questioned everything. Sharing often became uneasy for me. I worried too much about what other people thought of my decision to be a dabbler.

Dave opened our time with a moment of silence. And yes, he was there. (Are you starting to wonder when this guy sleeps?) I liked this quiet time, it reminded me of my daily meditation. When he introduced the topic of the movie—Rich: Maybe God has blessed us with everything we have so we can give to others—my heart leapt. It was as if I was meant to attend this morning.

A few years back, my sister, Laura, and I had discussed what we wanted to pass to our children. We hoped to empower them with the best qualities of our family. We had debated which ones were the most important. Our parents had taught us to have a strong work ethic, to care for the needs of others, to value security in the home, to make time for fun, and to honor the importance of traditions. I was excited for the video to start.

This short clip spoke to blessings in the Bible and how, in our modern world, they weren't as formal. That's a good start, I thought. I couldn't see the kids tolerating us if we laid hands on their heads. The film focused on some simple ones to say throughout your day. Waiting in line, you could silently pray for those nearby. When at a red light, a quick prayer could be said for all those on the road. The goal was to give a blessing in the moment. The video wrapped by acknowledging you only need one component, the spirit we brought to it.

I looked forward to hearing what everyone had to say on this topic. Starting on my right, a mother shared how she enjoyed her Mother's Day invocation. She's right I thought, our family always received special recognition on National Adoption Day. The priest invited families of adoption to stand after mass. Those around us laid their hands on our shoulders. It made me realize while adoption had become normal for us, it was a blessing. I recognized our family blessing didn't have to be a big announcement. It could be something that we named. As I mused on my new awareness, I quit listening to the others. Nudging me with her elbow, Jenni got my attention. It was my turn.

"Hmm, I want to recognize how family is a gift," I said. "A sharing of our values, like *we're Warners, not whiners.*"

"What values do you think are most important?" Mike asked.

"Well, being connected to one another, belonging," I said. "Kind of like what we have here."

"Sounds like camp is yours," Jenni said.

Mike and I smiled at one another. Choosing to attend camp, we had set our family blessing in motion. We only needed to recognize that camp was it. And we needed to live, breathe, and practice the camp spirit all year long. Looking forward to starting a list of all the ways I could bring the blessings of camp home, I knew just where to find a notebook. I hurried back to the cabin for it. (Little did I know this family blessing took hold and all three of our children became involved in camp in many ways over the years. I hope our kids have been able to give back to camp a portion of the gifts that they received.)

Writing Class

. . .

Sitting at the breakfast table, I looked at my plate of toast and scrambled eggs. I was excited for my next activity, a writing workshop, and didn't know if I had the stomach to eat. I had forgotten how much I wanted to write as a girl, and the sign-up sheet for this session reminded me of this dormant desire. As an elementary student, I wrote a lot. Ms. King, my fifth-grade teacher, told me I was an author. Of course, I believed her. Purchasing an extra spiral bound note-book each back-to-school season, I assumed one September one of my scribbles would hold a nugget. I frequently found myself on a quest for one brilliant sentence. Instead, the lined paper was used for science notes or math problems. Burying this seed of desire, I moved on with my homework and forgot. This session reignited my childhood aspiration. But first, breakfast.

Nibbling at a piece of toast, I pushed the scrambled eggs on my plate. Yup, nerves had chased my appetite away. I kept glancing at my watch in anticipation. Finally, breakfast was done, announcements were made, and I hurried to Alexander Hall. Tom, the leader of this activity, rocked in the glider chair. There was one other participant, Hope. Sitting beside her on the sofa, I noticed her leather-bound journal. Well, she looks serious, I thought. As she introduced herself, we learned she had been an English professor before chil-dren. Yes, I was intimidated. Reminding myself to have a beginner's mind, I settled in to learn.

"It's the three of us," Tom said. "Thanks for signing up!"

"I'm thrilled," Hope said. "I've recently returned to writing; this will be good exercise for me."

Great, I thought. The journal, the degree, the career—now, I'm really the newbie.

"Well, I have a lot to learn," I said. "I don't even know how to start."

"Let's do it," Tom said. "Here's the first step."

Our exercise was to list memories of our childhood for five minutes. I stared at the blank space. Picturing myself in my parents' home helped me. I started with one memory. Others followed, and soon my hand struggled to keep up with my brain. I wrote about moving next door to Jenni, my new school, the woods, sled riding–the memories flowed. The timer beeped, and we stopped. Then we read our items out loud. When I read "playing in the woods," Tom stopped me.

"Your face just lit up," he said. "Can you tell me more?"

I shared the details. In those summers of my youth, my brother and I woke, scooped handfuls of Lucky Charms straight from the box, and rushed outside. Rounding up our friends in the neighborhood, we took off for the day. Sometimes we challenged one another to see who could climb to the highest limb in the crab apple trees. Other days we would create another world by building a fortress. By far, my favorite was when we followed the creek to the waterfall.

Tom instructed, "Record all the details. Shut your eyes and imagine you're there, smack dab in the middle of the thickets. What were you wearing? What did you smell, hear, or feel?"

Writing as fast as I could, I outlined a typical day. The roaring of the waterfall thundered in my ears. Feeling its cool spray on my heated skin, I shivered. In my mind, I saw my younger self wearing my favorite swim club t-shirt. It was so soft; I wore it as often as possible. Feeling the delight again by putting myself back in the moment, I recalled how we counted on one another. I learned who took a dare—my brother. Which one of us always had snacks—Kurt. Who could talk me into anything—Jenni!

"Good," he said. "Now, go steal some quiet moments to turn all of this," he tapped his finger on my pad, "into a life essay."

"Are we able to meet later and workshop our pieces?" Hope asked.

"Excellent idea."

"What does that mean?" I asked.

"You read them out loud and then we offer advice," he answered.

"I'm in," said Hope.

"Okay, where and when?" I asked. I wasn't sure if I wanted to read my piece to them, but I couldn't be the party pooper. There were only the two of us, after all.

"Maybe after the book club discussion," Tom suggested.

I spent the rest of the morning thinking how as a kid, I stayed out until the streetlights came on. Listening for Jenni's dad's whistle, his staccato bursts interrupted our play, calling us home. Putting pen to paper helped me realize in real time my kids were having similar experiences here at camp. Discovering the crayfish creek and eagle's nest were their adventures. Instead of a whistle, they kept their ears peeled for the mealtime bell. Their days ended with them being dirty and hungry, like mine did decades ago.

Most kids don't go into the woods anymore. Their lives are full of sports, music lessons, and lots of other supervised activities. I was guilty of filling my kids' lives like this myself. Wanting to provide so much for them, I had deprived them of the chance to become independent. They needed to learn for themselves the pain of a crayfish pinch or mosquito bite. Most of all, how to rely on one another. I don't know if I would have made this connection as quickly if I hadn't jotted it all in my new notebook. Looking forward to working on this more, I realized writing wasn't so scary; it was a treat. One that I wanted to continue for another hour, so I headed to the patio of the snack bar.

Note: Hope continued her writing and has published several novels; my favorite is *Forever Music*.

· · ·

Michael's Lesson

When I arrived at the snack bar patio, I sat in what had become my favorite Adirondack chair. This seat had a view of the beach, playground, waterfront, and of course the lake. I settled in. Pulling my notebook from my backpack, I laid it on my lap. Digging in the bottom of the bag for a pen, I wanted to fill in some details on the waterfall hike. Tom and Hope had given me some tips on ways to improve my imagery. I wanted to capture the sensations. Going back in time, I felt the sun's rays on my bare shoulders. Memories of talking loudly over the sound of the water crashing on the rocks flooded my mind. What did we gab about all those years ago? I tried to imagine our voices. However, instead of hearing my childhood buddies, I heard Michael's angry voice. Snapping to attention, I saw a canoe had capsized.

Sigh, yes, it was my son. He and his two best buddies, Maria and Andy, bobbed beside their overturned canoe. As they angrily smacked water at one another, the lifeguards on the rescue boat approached. Gathering the oars, they righted the kids' boat. One at a time, they helped them back in. Handing them a bailer and their paddles, the lifeguards gave a demonstration of how to stroke. Then the waterfront staff returned to the dock.

I thought they should be towed to shore. They were

obviously having difficulty. The kids stared at one another. Finally, Andy dipped his paddle into the water and stroked, then Maria did the same, and finally Michael. Their craft strayed to the right, then the left, and then they all stopped. As they began to laugh at each other, I smiled. I silently rooted for them to work together. Trying again, they took turns paddling and attempting to correct the course. Finally, I saw their stroking become synchronized and the canoe cut smoothly through the water.

They had persevered and were successful. If staff had towed them to shore, they would not have learned this. I was glad I had sat on my hands and had not run down to the waterfront to assist them.

As they docked, they helped one another step to solid ground. Their faces shone with a sense of accomplishment, all grins. Shaking with laughter, they reenacted the capsize for their buds. After giving his life vest to Andy to return to the supply shed, Michael walked towards me.

"Did you see us capsize?"

"I did. What happened?"

"First, we were going in circles."

"Rats, I missed that part."

"Then, we tried to change seats, so we were more balanced, and we fell out."

"That's what I saw, all of you in the water."

"Well, the staff insisted we could paddle a canoe

once we stopped blaming each other." Andy and Maria called to him to hurry.

"Got to go, we're going to try archery, now." As he ran down the hill to catch them, I thought about how their boating experience could be a metaphor for friendships. Everyone had to paddle. If one friend did all the work, the relationship would be off balance. It was also important to pitch in and bail any water the canoe was taking on. Whenever there were leaks, it's key that each person shares the responsibility of bailing. And sometimes you switched who was steering. Ultimately, it was critical to relax and have fun. Once they quit blaming one another and were encouraging, they maneuvered the boat flawlessly.

It reminded me of a quote by Helen Keller, "Alone we can do so little, together we can do so much." I'm sure I'm overthinking this, but I believed they were lucky to have learned this lesson at such a young age. Their relationships should be stronger from their experience. I returned to my writing and tried to incorporate this lesson of friendship into my story of my lifelong friends. Focused on one who has traveled by my side to this day, Jenni, I had enough time before dinner to transcribe a very rough draft.

The Bears

·   ·   ·

After dinner, the kids convinced us to allow them to skip the children's activity. They were scheduled to go on a hayride while we went to Café Night. This event was a performance for adults only. It was the one evening we had to ourselves, and Mike and I looked forward to it. Some parents shared that we could leave our kids in the game room. Giving them instructions not to leave, we left them at a table putting a puzzle together. I still worried. My gut told me this plan might not be the best one. After all, the hayride was supervised by staff. However, I was coerced into going along. Apparently, peer pressure didn't end after high school. *Everyone met at the snack bar afterward, anyway.*

Taking the long way to Alexander Hall, the venue for Café Night, Mike and I walked by the lake and watched the sun set. I was at peace and pleased with how each day provided an opportunity for me to loosen the reins a little bit more. Arriving at the hall, we joined the line. Energy coursed through the adults. The past four evenings, well past midnight, we had heard staff practicing into the wee hours of the morning. We were buzzed to see the result. Jenni and Scott arrived to join us, and Scott said, "We saw a mother bear and two cubs next to your porch."

"Oh no, the kids," I said.

"They'll be fine," Jenni said. "Meet them when the wagon comes back."

"They didn't go," I said. "C'mon," I turned to Mike. "They can't leave the snack bar."

He was ten steps ahead of us. We took off after him. Immediately, my thoughts turned to blame. I should not have ignored my gut warning. This is exactly why I liked to manage as much as possible. Thoughts raced through my head, like *Which one of my kids is the slowest? How far is the closest hospital? Can I take on a bear?* Arriving at a dark snack bar, Mike flipped on the lights. The kids were not sitting at the table piecing together the jigsaw. I was angry. Torn between fear for their safety and wanting to kill them for not listening, I started to cry. My flight response was always stronger than my fight one. Jenni clutched my arm, "Let's go." She pulled me in the direction of our cabin.

"We should find your kids, fast."

The guys raced to catch the hay wagon hoping the kids had a change of mind. All I knew of bears was what I watched on nature shows—bears in full aggressive mode protecting their babies. What chance did little kids have against razor sharp teeth and powerful claws? I visualized the bears dragging our kids into the woods. Before my mind quit rambling with "what if?" scenarios, we were at our dark and empty cabin. No bears and no kids.

"Now what?"

"We keep looking," Jenni said. "Let's go find the guys." Running down the hill, we saw the hayride leaving the parking lot. Mike shook his head at me. They were not on the wagon.

"I'm ringing the emergency bell," I said.

"Wait," he said. "I have an idea. Let's look for well-lit cabins, maybe we'll see kids' heads in the shadows."

"What?" I asked.

"Well, no one should be in their rooms, right?" he said. "So, if we see lights on and a bunch of heads, most likely it's the kids." (Reminder: they were all young, so their heads barely rose above the windowsills.) I didn't want it to, but Mike's idea made sense.

We hustled along the trail where only a few of the cabins were lit. As all four of us stared at each cabin for signs of life, shadows danced by the windows of one. Dashing to the cabin, we banged on the door. The girls' new friend, Rachel, opened it. The kids jumped on beds squealing with laughter. When they saw our four worried faces, they silenced. I was uncertain if I should hug them or shake them. Jenni and Scott slipped away.

"You're supposed to be in the snack bar," Mike said. The kids stared at his clenched teeth.

"Becca and Rachel invited us for candy," Mia said. Stuffing a red rope of licorice in her mouth, she was unfazed.

"You scared us," I said.

"Bears are roaming the grounds," Mike said.

"Bears, cool!" Michael said. He tossed an M&M in the air and caught it in his mouth.

"If you accidentally got between the mother and her kids, there's no telling what could have happened," I said. They were not grasping the seriousness of the situation.

"There were babies?" Megan asked. "Can we go look for them?" She took a big bite of a chocolate cookie.

"No!" I said. Sighing, I looked at Mike. "I don't think we can leave them alone."

"We promise we're not going anywhere," Michael said. "Look at all the goods." He waved his arm at the shelf of cookies and candy.

"I don't know," I said.

"Please, let us stay," Mia and Megan begged. This entire time, their friends sat on a cot snacking on Doritos. It all looked innocent enough. And, I had a clear line of vision from Alexander Hall.

"Ok," I said. "Do. Not. Leave."

"Or else," Mike added. He scowled for effect.

We rushed to Café Night and settled into the chairs Scott and Jenni had saved for us. She whispered we only missed one song. Staff sang the top hits of my high school years, the eighties. My favorite "Girls Just Want to Have Fun" by Cindi Lauper had me chair dancing, but I never relaxed. Peering outside, I saw they were back to jumping on beds.

"Look at them," I said. "They're really pissing me off."

"Just leave it and enjoy the show."

I was angry I was talked into leaving them, got scared out of my wits, and then everyone else returned to normal life. Losing command of their safety made me wish I had stood my ground. I clenched my fists on my lap. Grinding my teeth, my mind went into overdrive thinking trusting anyone other than myself to raise the kids wasn't in the best interests of my family. This is exactly why I scheduled every minute for them. So, no one gets in trouble or hurt. I had a conversation in mind to have with Mike, but it would have to wait until the staff was done performing.

Note: at the time of this incident, I didn't make the connection that after 9/11 our sense of security had been derailed. It's possible this anxiety stemmed from that trauma.

Everyone Pitches In—The Camp Spirit

The hour of entertainment ended, and staff received a standing ovation. Then, in typical camp fashion, everyone assisted with cleaning. Stacking chairs, we helped get the auditorium in order. We knew the performers were tired and still had snack bar duty before they could retire. The last seat was stacked, the floor was swept, and the place was spotless for tomorrow's activities.

Humming to my favorite song of the evening, "Don't You (Forget about Me)" by Simple Minds, helped me relax from the earlier stress of the bears. I was trying to allow the kids to grow into self-sufficient people. As difficult as it was, I knew they needed to test boundaries and face the consequences. But bears? I shuddered.

"I hope the kids survive our parenting," I said. "Long enough to become teens and be on staff."

"I think that would be awesome. This seems like a really special place. And our parenting is well above average, just like our kids," he said with his usual big grin.

"Really? This is not the first time they've been on their own."

"We are giving them direction with minimal guidance."

"I can't decide what takes more effort, hovering or practicing benign neglect."

"Hey, most of these young adults were raised here," Mike said. "And they are amazing."

"Yeah, it's tiring being an authoritarian," I said.

"You'll see, before you know it our kids will be on the stage, performing on Café Night."

I wasn't sure I believed him. Keeping the smile on my face I did my best to act like nothing was bothering me. My attitude was one thing I could still control. It seemed we had moved from organizing our kids' time to a free for all. I wasn't sure that I liked the direction we were headed. If I knew one thing from running with Tracy, she would allow me to share my struggle on our run in the morning. Hoping to leave these thoughts until then, we marshaled the kids to bed.

THURSDAY

<u>Freedom to Run</u>

Sunlight flickered through the leaves of the oak, danced across my eyelids, and woke me. I rolled away from the window. Annoyed, I struggled to wake from that in-between state. I hadn't slept well as my brain kept thinking about how I needed to be more on top of the kids. I thought I was okay with not being a helicopter mom, but perhaps I could lean on "trust but verify." Moving from juggling too much to total freedom bumped along in an uncomfortable way.

Opening my eyes, I glanced at the clock on the side table. Yup, I overslept and was late to meet Tracy for our run! I threw off the covers, brushed my teeth, shoved on running shoes, and set a hat on my head. Flying off the porch, I tried to catch her. I really wanted to talk with her about our struggle to find balance. I knew if she listened as I spoke my concerns out loud that a solution might appear. Running at camp had been easy with her. We showed up, ran, talked, and made one another feel better physically and mentally.

Scrambling, I attempted to stay upright as I gathered speed. My arms flailed as I maintained balance over craggy rocks and tree roots. Nearing our usual meeting spot, I didn't see Tracy. I missed her. Bummed, I slowed at the office. I noticed the staff had gathered. Some of them bounced with energy and others rubbed sleepers from their eyes. Dave cradled the U.S. flag. I stopped in my tracks and changed my mind. Deciding to join them, I merged with the ranks. I had participated in many flag raising ceremonies as a Girl Scout, but I had never attended one here. I wasn't sure what drew me to pause and change my plans, but I felt an immediate sense of reverence walking with the small crowd.

We headed toward the dining hall in single file. Stepping through the dewy grass, I found some families already standing in a circle. I took an available spot and glanced around. I identified veterans, military academy students, and parents with youngsters—I knew from the activity board children were especially eager to sign on for the flag raising ceremony. How wonderful parents instilled this respect and appreciation for our country and freedoms.

This was a fantastic way for me to devote five

minutes in gratitude before running. In her article, "Defying a Cultural Taboo, Saudi Women Are Running —and They're Not Going to Stop" (*Runners' World,* Sept. 7, 2018) Michelle Hamilton writes about the challenges some people face because of their race, religion, or other identifiers. One of the women quoted in the article stated, "Being able to run is freedom, you gain self-esteem and confidence. We should all work to provide this opportunity to everyone." I understood the importance of her statement from experience. We had moved often and running with a local club became a way for me to integrate in my new neighborhood. Reflecting on the article, the message had weighed heavy on my heart that not everyone had this privilege. Although I didn't quite know what to do with my new understanding of the challenges others faced, I thought I could at least pause and be grateful.

Dave and two kids snapped the flag into the rope's clips. His large hands guided the rope as the smaller hands of the children pulled in sync. Quieting, our eyes followed the flag to the top of the pole where it unfurled. He asked for a moment of silence. I lowered my eyes and prayed for all people of the world—that they could know this power. I had leaned on running as my main form of exercise for so long I had started to take it for granted.

My devotion to running started at camp. Kelli, my childhood camp bestie, was on a cross-country club, and she invited me to run with her. When I couldn't keep pace with her, another camper, Mr. Crouse, persuaded me to run with him. It wasn't until I naively signed on for a 10K in high school that I learned how strong I was. I liked it. Appearing at the start line back then in my Converse canvas sneakers brought a few curious looks. My swim coach's face had registered his surprise to see me toeing the start line.

"I didn't know you were a runner, Maria," Coach Thomas said.

"I'm not, I'm hoping to stay in shape for the swim club, Coach," I replied. The race started and I took off too fast. Coach ran by my side and urged me to keep his pace. He talked to me the entire six miles and gave me advice on how to handle the hills. When I crossed the finish line, he congratulated me and suggested I invest in a pair of running shoes. At the time I didn't appreciate how he had put his race aside to make sure mine was a success.

My affair with running continued. I knew if I could run on little training and without proper footwear, I had the mental portion solved. Once I learned how to train, I took on longer distances. The sense of accomplishment of being disciplined and consistent carried into all areas of my life. I often reminded myself and the children that life was a marathon not a sprint. When difficulties arose, it was important to keep putting one foot in front of the other and move forward. Ha, I should take my own advice. Trust that camp would get us on the right path. That I needed to relax.

We followed the silence with the Pledge of Allegiance, our right hands on our hearts. As I recited the pledge, a sense of deep pleasure overcame me. I thanked God I belonged to a camp that valued family, freedom, and country. In my mind, running and the flag raising all came together to represent something bigger than my little three-mile jaunt. Deciding to dedicate my run to those that serve, whether it was their country, camp, or as running mentors, I dashed off with a spring in my step.

Passing the staff lodge, I considered how those young adults devoted their summers to serving families. I hoped our children volunteered and worked here. I knew they would learn personal responsibility, the value of demanding work, and the reward of selfless giving. I said a little prayer for all the staff. Continuing through the woods, I raced through the covered kissing bridge. As I ran by the cottages, I thought of how we—campers from around the country—united to soothe a child when they fell, cheered one another during games, and enjoyed each other's company over a milkshake. We embraced the shared belief of building strong families. I practiced on the campers as I passed. *Stay safe, may you have fun, hope you feel like you belong...*

I never caught Tracy and ran solo, but I didn't feel alone. My thoughts and prayers kept me company. I reflected on how I kept beating myself up for every little mistake I made along the way of parenting. And I needed to cut myself some slack. Of course, the kids weren't going to listen to us all the time. Hadn't I just spent the entire run thinking of how wonderful these camp families and staff members all were? Why did I think our family was so different? Our kids would be fine. These little hiccups were seeds in the watermelon, as Mike reminded me after breakfast when I shared with him my worries.

Spit out the seeds and pay them no mind, focus on the meat of the fruit.

We continued our conversation over coffee while the kids went to group. Like our complementary skills in the kitchen, he reminded me that our parenting tactics balanced just as nicely.

"I'm really good at structure and planning," I said.

"I know, and it helps, but we also need to teach the kids to test boundaries," he said.

"Like letting them wander all over camp?"

"Yes, it's safe, there are lots of adults keeping an eye on them."

"And do you think we're moving towards a more balanced family?"

"Of course, I already see improvements in how they help one another, assist at meals, and look after other's little ones."

"Great points, I'll loosen up." I liked that he kept me focused on how camp was more than a vacation. This week accomplished a lot for us, as my parents had suggested.

The Triathlon

Daily, Jenni hovered after lunch, pestering me to check the bulletin board and take on the triathlon. I ignored her. I had already tried a few new things this week. How many times in one week do I have to make myself uncomfortable?

"C'mon, let's go," she said. She guided me with one firm hand on my shoulder and another on my elbow. Arriving at the registration sheet, she said "See, there it is–the triathlon."

There were two events, solo competitor or as a relay. Most of the solo athletes were male. I was surprised to see Mike was one of the entrants. Then I realized I shouldn't have been as he *was* trying to fit in as many activities as possible.

"I'll be the only woman," I said.

"Maria this is your lane, you've got this."

"Hmm, it's a kayak-bike-run. If it were a swim, I'd kick butt."

"Maybe we should do the relay entry?" she asked. "Remember, this is for fun."

"Ok, I'll do the run piece."

Even when we were kids, she could talk me into

trying anything once. Like when we roller-skated in the grocery store and got scolded by the manager. Or climbed the public pool fence and snuck in a midnight swim. I supposed this is what made our relationship so exceptional. She had outrageous ideas and I was game. We cracked each other into pieces giggling over our antics. She often reminded me that "this is how memories get made."

"I'll bike and Scott will kayak." She completed our entry. While looking for Scott to let him know what we'd volunteered him for, we saw Mike in the sundry shop. He purchased a pair of Croakies, the neoprene holders that keep your glasses strapped to your face in perilous conditions. I wasn't sure why he needed them; it wasn't like we were going white water rafting.

"Watcha doing?" I asked.

"These will come in handy for the tri; I have a special strategy."

"We're doing the tri, too," I said. "We also have a plan."

"Relax and enjoy the journey," Jenni reminded me.

Leaving Mike, we found Scott and let him know we volunteered him for the kayaking. We walked to the grass by the dock and watched staff line the boats, rope off the transition area for the bikers, and draw chalk arrows on the run course. As everyone trickled in to compete, I noticed there weren't enough kayaks. Learning we needed to go off in heats, I realized we were in the same one as Mike. I felt tricked. Going from being the only team to now competing against the individuals made me a little anxious.

I repeated to myself, *relish this new experience.* However, the phrase became, *go your hardest and do your part not to lose*!

"I think there's something wrong with me," I said. "I really want to win."

"Do your best," Scott said. "And have fun!" Flexing his biceps, he posed as if he was competing in a bodybuilding contest. A whistle blast meant it was time to gather for instructions.

Mike stared into space as if in a trance. I thought he was visualizing his strategy. Scott stood next to him in a sprinter pose. Jenni and I rolled our eyes.

"These two," she said. "Look at them."

Mike adjusted the new strap for his glasses. The horn sounded and off they went. The pack was so tight, we quickly lost track of who was who.

"I can't tell who is in the lead," I said.

"Oh shoot, someone capsized," Jenni said. "There goes the rescue speedboat."

"If staff assists them, are they disqualified?"

"Hey, Ms. Cutthroat, let's make sure they're safe?"

"Oh yeah, that too."

"Here comes Scott."

He jumped from the kayak, dropped his paddle, and raced toward us. He ran with Jenni to her bike and helped her secure the relay band on her wrist. She started to peddle through the woods toward the kissing bridge turnaround. Joining me, Scott put his hands on his knees and gasped for air. While patting him on the back, Mike yelled at us as he sprinted to his bike.

"Epic fail!"

Scott shared, "Mike was way in front. Next thing I knew he was in the water trapped under his kayak." He paused. "I was torn between making sure he was safe or beating him back."

"He looks okay," I said. I guessed those Croakies did come in handy.

A staffer called, "First biker returning." I got ready to take the relay band from Jenni. It was Mike!

"Hey, where's my teamie?"

He ditched the bike and headed on the run. "Na-na, you can't catch me."

Coated in mud, Jenni appeared. Red faced from her all-out effort she held the band to me. Grabbing it, I turned to sprint after Mike. Hearing Scott ask her if she was okay, I realized I should have checked on her. But Mike was getting away.

The first section of the run was a steep hill. Rounding the corner, his sprint became a walk. Hmm, do I pass him or inspire him, I wondered. My feelings were mixed. Competitor Maria would nudge him on my way by; caring Maria should persuade him to pace with me. What a dilemma! I only had a few seconds to decide.

"Let's go." Even though my drive to do my best was in full force, I wanted him to do his best, too. It's common in races to push one another. I often trailed someone to help regulate my pace. Sometimes others used me as their rabbit for motivation. Mike increased his speed.

His gulps for air became deeper, and I thought I had the edge. Beads of sweat dripped down my back. I anticipated flying over the finish line first. We had a steep hill before the final yards. The finish, in sight, was a roll of toilet paper stretched over the line for the winner to break. A few bystanders said, "It's neck and neck. Look at them go!"

I sensed Mike behind me but didn't want to turn my head to note his position. Their comments confirmed it was close. Lack of oxygen burned my lungs. Scott and Jenni were jumping with enthusiasm for me to race faster. In my peripheral vision, I saw Mike stride for stride with me. Only three more feet, a stitch in my side grew stronger, stomach juices gurgled as if I was going to hurl, and then we broke the toilet paper tape together.

"So exciting," murmured through the bystanders. I squatted and put my head between my knees. Allowing for the blood to flow back to my brain, my huffing slowed. I looked at Mike who was laying in the grass, wiped.

"Some ending, huh," I said.

He lifted his finger to give him one more minute to recover. The other participants arrived. Another athlete was soaked. Someone had blown a shoe and ran barefoot. We waited for Mike to catch his breath so he could share his capsize story with us.

"Well," he said. "I planned to paddle to the buoy first and block everyone."

"So, what happened?" I asked.

"He was first," Scott said. "And then he was last."

"Yup, I overdid the back paddling. My kayak shot to the sky, and I slid off the back."

"How did you get back on?" Jenni asked. We looked at one another to hear if he was assisted.

"I was told to straddle the rear with my legs and mount it from behind," Mike said. He imitated how he accomplished reentry onto his kayak.

"Glad I didn't wait," Scott said. "My eyes don't need to see you in that position."

"Family camp," I said. Whenever there were children nearby and we needed to watch our mouths, to keep it G rated, someone said "family camp" under their breath. Like on the volleyball court, when someone made a mistake and wanted to swear, they'd mutter our code phrase instead.

We thanked staff for hosting the event and let them know we thought it should stay on the schedule. Walking away to stretch our legs Mike recapped our fun.

"Another awesome story," he said. "Humiliation and laughter all wrapped with a bow." He tied some toilet paper in the shape of one around his neck. Later, we shared the funnier moments of the tri with our tablemates, Jodi and Doug, holding them captive with our reenactment. (Well, that is what I tell myself!)

Teasing one another as we described our own elements, we recaptured our joy; it wasn't all about competing to beat each other to the finish line. Joking and having a sense of humor has kept us together for over a decade (and now three). Racing together was another way we shared our commitment to look out for one another. So much so, I loved Mike enough to hold back in the run, so we tied. At the last second, I was reminded of our first race together, how Mike waited for me. In the spirit of getting to the finish line together, whatever age and shape we were in, I checked my competitiveness.

Speaking of competition, while I mused at the dining table, Mike had headed to the microphone during post-meal announcements. I just caught the last part of his statement. He planned on hosting a music game in the snack bar in the evening. All were invited to test their music skills in a friendly diversion, since the evening activities looked to be rained out.

Mike's *Name that Tune* Night

After dinner, the clouds opened and it started to pour, again. Curling under a blanket, back in our cabin, I waited for the pounding on the roof to stop.

Surrounded by the thick smell of soaking wet forest, I wondered what was taking Mike so long. He went to the office over an hour ago to use their Wi-Fi for his music downloads. And, to get quarters for the dryer. Where was he? Now *I* had to go into the rain.

Peeling myself from under the warm layers, I grumbled wishing for the rain to stop, forever. I knew letting the weather get the best of me, which I had no power over, wasn't particularly useful. I needed to dry our clothes, so I could be layered and warm. Slipping into rain boots, I took some bills to exchange for coins to the office.

Closing the office door behind me, I approached the counter. Cindy scraped together some quarters as I wasn't the only one who had requested change. The more it rained, the faster we all went through our clean clothes. As I turned to leave, I saw Mike in the lobby. Humming, he mouthed the words to the song playing on his computer.

I tapped him on the shoulder to get his attention. Even though I knew what he was up to, there was an unspoken rule allowing you to harass someone if you saw them using technology. Lack of tech connection was one of the reasons we adored camp. The cell service was nonexistent, and the Wi-Fi was reserved for the office. Earlier in the week, Mike had heard you could catch a mobile signal in the corner of the overlook tower. So, we hiked the mountain, climbed the stairs to the platform, and he held his phone in the air trying to get service. He found a connection. Starting to listen to his messages, he was embarrassed when some hikers approached the tower and called to him.

"Hey, Mike, watcha doing?" After their teasing, he put the phone away and resolved work could wait.

"Don't make me find your buddies to pester you," I said.

"I'm downloading 80s songs and creating a contest for *Name that Tune*." At home, he liked to create a music guessing game to play with our friends. When the rain started, Mike let everyone know he planned to put a session together.

"Oh, can I see your selections?" I asked.

"Hey, stop it, that is cheating," he said.

"You know I'm a horrible guesser. Come on, please."

"I'll give you one hint, there may be some weather-related choices." He winked. Shutting his laptop he said, "It's time to go set up my Bluetooth speaker in the snack bar."

"Let me start the dryer, then I'll be right there."

"Hurry, I hope it's crowded." He was right; the rain had restarted, and the outdoor activities had been canceled. Everyone tended to gravitate to the snack bar during a storm.

I reached the laundry room just as Hope came out with her own basket.

"Maria, don't you need to get to Mike's game?"

Ever since Hope and I had bonded over writing, I bumped into her everywhere. I liked the familiarity we had developed in a brief period. It reminded me of when you move to a new neighborhood, of that instant when you were acquainted enough with someone to say hello at the grocery store. That was the moment you belonged to your new neighborhood.

"Yes, one more load of clothes to move," I said. "Shall we be a team?"

"Yeah, but I never remember song titles."

"Me neither, I don't follow music like Mike."

"His enthusiasm is contagious."

"It's definitely one of his passions. Save me a spot. I'll hurry."

I thought about her comment as I inserted the quarters into the dryer slots. She was right, Mike shined when he talked about music. Songs connected us in so many ways. Our kids had bedtime favorites. They liked "Old McDonald had a Farm." We had concerts we attended, always going to see U2 when they toured. Like the songs at Café Night, I could be transported back to freshman year in college with one verse. "Forever Young," by Alphaville came to mind. Drawing my attention to Mike's zeal, Hope helped me grasp that it was more than a pastime for him.

I entered the game room side of the snack bar, and Hope motioned for me to sit beside her. Taking the empty chair, I looked around the crowded area. Every table was filled with eager adults. Everyone was good humored—cabin fever left behind. We enlisted Jenni and Sara to complete our squad.

Mike started the game and his enthusiasm extended to all of us. Allowing kids to join in the entertainment, he let them choose the next ditty. They pressed the start button so we could hear a few seconds of music. Whispering, we collaborated on our guesses. After hitting the pause button, he asked the captain of each table to announce their answers. Keeping score of a point for both artist and song track, he updated the totals. Everyone had a chance to guess correctly.

Even if you stunk, like we did, we earned points for creativity. For example, we wrote U2 when we didn't have a clue, and we scored bonus marks for sucking-up to the DJ. (You can figure out Mike's favorite band.) Others had to do the Rick Astley dance from his "Never Gonna Give You Up" video to get bonus points and catch up to the leaders. After the last round, the victorious players won the prize. Milkshakes!

Afterward, I heard the others comment on what a fun time they had. One couple said they didn't feel like leaving their cabin due to the rain. Then they recalled Mike was putting this game together. *What a terrific thing to do on a rainy night,* they said. They, like me, could have easily stayed in and been alone. I was glad Hope helped me recognize how important this activity was to Mike. And by the end of the game, the rain had stopped. Purchasing milkshakes for the winning team, he slapped them jovially on their backs. Then we all went outside to yet another music activity.

· · ·

Note: Mike continued this tradition throughout the years of camp. Keeping his annual list, he didn't repeat any of the songs. He also recalled who was a ringer in the past, so he sought to mix his choices to give everyone a chance. I saw the amount of time he took to create his lists. He enjoyed every minute of his preparation, managing the game, and the fun from being together.

Troubadours…The Music Continues

After we left the snack bar, we found space around the firepit. Beginner and experienced guitarists gathered and tuned their instruments. The crackling heat of the fire warmed us as the night was chilly. The next hour was devoted to perusing the Troubadour songbook and its collection of folk and rock anthems. We started with "Take it Easy" by the Eagles and then moved to "American Pie" by Don McLean.

Music was an important chunk of our week—singing grace before eating, while walking on trails, and now at the firepit. Song was another way of storytelling. Some were pure fun, with moving body parts and lots of action. Like our "repeat after me" tunes. Everyone drummed their fingers, stomped their feet, and clapped their hands. Others were gospel hymns expressing gratitude before our meals. Some of those were solemn and a few were goofy. The fact that we all took turns requesting our favorites was the best feature of Troubadour. There was the heat of the fire and friendship to warm our hearts while waiting for our turn.

As the evening wore on, a magical quality hung in the air. We were participating in a tradition that had been going on long before our arrival and would continue after our departure. I was learning that a place can be spiritual for many reasons. As a young adult, I knew camp was special but had never quite been able to explain why. Now, I decided these notes we were singing circled around us enveloping us with all the love and kinship we shared.

All those who came before us and those on the same path, here at camp, helped me. Our shared community provided a safe place for me to explore how I wanted to be with myself, family, and friends. I was learning I didn't have to do it alone, or by the book. There were others here at camp invested in our family's success.

The snack bar lights dimmed, the guitars were put in their cases, and the songbooks were gathered. The embers died. No one wanted to leave first. This was one of those extraordinary times in life you don't want to end because the emotions are so powerful. Like a wedding reception or a graduation party—pleased to be part of the celebration of what it took to get to that point and hopeful for the future. Soon, however, the ashes dimmed and the cold seeped into our bones. It was time to go. The melancholy of understanding we had less than thirty-six hours left at camp settled into my thoughts.

After arriving at the cottage, we tucked in the kids, and they murmured how tomorrow was our last full day. They struggled to stay awake and make the evening last. I knew the sadness they were experiencing. It hurt to leave, as it had for me as a youngster. You couldn't have the pleasure of the week without the sadness. I vowed to make the most of the last day even if it rained nonstop.

Lying in bed, I reviewed the whole week. I started to think about how each family brings a little bit of their specialness to the camp world. For example, one family's life centered around horses. Kathy is a large animal vet, and her husband Kerry runs and judges at horse shows around the country. They brought their expertise to camp by assisting in the horse barn and with the rides. Every family had unique gifts that made for a positive community.

Camp had worked its magic. Little by little, by making new friends and trying different activities I had opened my heart. Worrying over giving the kids "it all" had been replaced by giving them what I now knew they really needed. Time with friends, us, by themselves, downtime, etc. I had one more day to see what else I could take home with me.

FRIDAY

<u>On Being</u>

After breakfast, wanting to savor everything, I tried to make time stand still. I walked to the water's edge, sat on a low bench, and dipped my toes in. I lifted my gaze to the peak of the mountain. Resting my eyes on the crown, I remembered hiking to the top as an adolescent for an overnight. It had been a rite of passage to slumber there beneath the stars for our last evening together. We built a fire, positioned our sleeping bags near it, and spoke of our dreams into the early morning hours. One of my aspirations had been to work at camp. While that didn't come true, I was given this gift of returning with my family.

"Penny for your thoughts?" Charlie asked. Scooching, I made space for him.

"I used to sleep at the top of that mountain with the teens."

"Ah, the intimacy of being with your buds."

"I miss all the free time with my friends."

"Yup, I know what you mean, conversations going in all kinds of directions." Charlie leaned back and settled in.

"Everyone figuring out life, instead of reading about it."

"I think that is why Tracy and I like camp so much, revisiting what is important."

"I've learned to relax and let the kids find their own path." I took a deep breath when I shared that thought.

"Camp lets us care for children without too much structure."

"Yeah, my kids seem to be happy."

"Well, when I see them, they appear to be having a blast." Charlie pointed to them as they ran by.

"I know, darn them, for not needing my guidance."

"You're doing a fantastic job." He smiled at me.

"Well, Mike and I have a few things to talk over on our drive home."

"Like allowing the kids to sing on their chairs at mealtime?" He raised his eyebrows.

"Well, maybe only at home."

We laughed and then settled into silence. I thought of all the things I wanted to bring home. I assumed Charlie was doing the same. We shared the bench in solitude for thirty minutes. We were two friends sitting comfortably, lost in our thoughts. Simply being while we carved space to care for one another.

Across the Lake Swim

A waterfront staffer announced it was time for the Across-the-Lake swim. This was one activity I didn't need to be called twice for.

"Charlie, I've treasured this time with you, but I gotta go," I said. "I've been looking forward to this swim."

"Go, go on."

I walked toward the boats. Twenty of us gathered on the metal dock. This event, another rite of passage like the spring hike, was a five-hundred-yard swim to the island and back. This plunge off the dock was enjoyed by all ages and abilities.

I have always been partial to this event. In fact, I owned it as a youth. The swim became "my thing." In the past, I'd "won" it many times. It wasn't supposed to be a competition, but I trained at home each year to ensure I reached the island first. Even when the water temperature was below sixty degrees, I still signed on to swim and dominate.

But now, at age forty, I felt a little stupid. On the first day of signups, I struggled as to whether to partici-pate or not. I stood in front of the sheet and wondered what was wrong with me. Why would I want to come in first in a friendly swim that included twelve-year-olds? Maybe it was time to hang up my swim cap. I worried I was too old to come in first. What would people think of me when I arrived in my competition swimsuit and goggles?

Then, in a moment of clarity, I to swim alongside everyone and cheer them on. When I was eleven, one of the dads, Mr. Johnson, challenged me to try and keep up with him. He swam in front of me, and I benefited by drafting off of him. Trying my best to catch him, I stayed on his feet. Every stroke I took almost touched his toes. It spurred me on to reach longer, breathe less often, and kick harder. When he finished ahead of me, he urged me to continue practicing so I could beat him the next summer. I swam consistently over the year, becoming stronger. The next summer I beat him. It was terrific to realize my hard work had the result that I pursued. I decided to channel him and provide words of inspiration to the other swimmers.

Yes, I was set to transition to coach. I signed my name at the bottom of the list, understanding the lifeguards would call us in order. I thought by jumping in last my competitive fire would be contained.

"Who's ready?" Chris, the waterfront director, called. Peeling off our warm layers of sweat clothes, we dropped them to the dock. Their colors stood in contrast with the gray steel like a rainbow against storm clouds. I shivered, goosebumps coating my arms and legs.

We listened to the sounds of the final bocce ball, basketball, and volleyball competitions chorusing behind us as we stared at the island. Some of us had Speedo suits and others wore recreational ones. We ran the gamut from kids under ten to "kids" in our forties and fifties. We differed in age, but our desire to successfully navigate the long distance, waves, and chilly water was the same. No one wanted a lifeguard to rescue them. And a rescued swimmer was forced to ride the pontoon boat back to the dock. I mentally prepared for the challenge. But, the island, our goal, looked like a wafer floating in the distance.

I decided to begin my cheering while waiting for the start. "Awesome, you're not wearing a life vest," I said to Jenni's daughter, Josie. At seven, she must have passed the deep-water test.

"I'm doing the round trip without any help."

"Emily, you're wearing a club suit; you're going to be amazing," I added. Emily, eight, smiled and pulled her yellow cap tighter over her ears. It struck me both girls were younger than I had been for my inaugural lake swim.

The sun-warmed metal heated my feet. The temperature was in the low seventies and there was a wispy breeze coming off the dam to our right. The gust created wavelets dancing on the normally calm surface. I reminded myself to breathe on my left. No need to swallow any white caps. Bouncing on my toes, nervous energy kept me in motion. It took pluck to swim open water, with no lane ropes or pool sides to grab. I worked on my jitters by doing a pre-race jiggle.

I tugged my straps as they dug into my shoulders; I continued to follow the advice of my high school captain decades later. A tight suit reduced drag and enabled me to be faster. Okay, fine, so I still respected the prep for a competitive race. It didn't mean anything. Really, this wasn't the Olympics after all.

The lifeguards boarded their kayaks so they could guide us to the island. Many of the parents were on the pontoon boat. They cheered for each one of us as Chris called our names.

I adjusted my goggles, gulped, and plunged off the edge. Like a punch to my chest, the cold sucked the air out of my lungs. Surfacing, I struggled to catch my breath. Gasping while treading water, I steadied my breathing and cleared my goggles.

I knew they would not help me see through the opaque bluish-green water, but goggles were part of the uniform. Frankly, I didn't mind not seeing well, as I knew I could encounter fish, snapping turtles, and maybe a snake along the way. The thought of meeting an animal persuaded me to catch the rest of the swimmers. I didn't think I should be all alone behind everyone! I don't like snakes. Isn't there safety in numbers?

Lowering my face, I raised my legs and started to kick. I propelled forward. My right elbow exited at my waist, driving my right hand past my ear, and then dropped in front of my eyes. Then my left arm motioned the same movement. Muscle memory returned and my body relaxed into its rhythm. Noticing the sun rays glittering below the surface, I lingered on the spot warmed by the light. I lifted my head and noted my position. I had stopped short of swimming right past a cluster of swimmers. Treading water for a few more gulps of air, I cheered them on a bit, "Fabulous job! Looking good!" Lowering my head, I continued, proud of restraining myself from going all out and passing them by without a word. As a youthful swimmer, I had saved all my breath for the event. As the mature adult that I was, I used my energy to urge on others.

Right stroke, left stroke, I remembered to take in air on the left to avoid the waves. Again, I looked to note my position. Oops, I had reached the middle of the pack. I had meant to loiter behind everyone and inspire them. I'll dog paddle alongside and cheer on them, too. "Great job everyone!"

While I enjoyed my time cheerleading the slower swimmers, I watched the first crew stretch their lead. Somewhere within, a spark was ignited, and I didn't want it quenched. Oh no, they don't. I had to catch them.

I stroked and kicked with a little more effort. I settled into this pattern, relishing this euphoric feeling of invincibility, no discomfort, and a complete loss of time. Entering the zone, I became conscious I was doing my best. And I was leading!

My distance grew. I lifted my head to take a big breath and realized the lead kayak was having to leave some others behind to catch up to me. I was being stupid. By separating myself, I was potentially putting the others in danger. I was *winning*, but at what cost? I had become a competitive jerk. What happened to me wanting to cheer everyone on? I was disappointed in myself. Forgetting I had wanted to inspire campers to cross together, I had turned it into my own personal competition. How easily I had slipped back into only thinking of myself. Was this a value I wanted the kids to learn from me? Thank goodness they were not witnessing their mother's actions.

Treading water, I waited for the others to arrive. This gave me time to reflect on how quickly my plan had turned south. Returning to my earlier form, I complimented each swimmer as they reached me. Everyone popped from the water with a smile of pride. I was embarrassed of my behavior. I should have been more supportive. The pontoon boat arrived full of clapping parents.

"Emily did an outstanding job," I called to her mother.

"She likes being part of a club."

Ouch! Her comment, which was innocent, made me feel even worse. I had not been a good teammate. Squishing my toes in the muck, I shook my arms to keep them warm, and then lowered my goggles. Blowing their whistles, the lifeguards indicated it was time to go back. As amazing as the swim over had been, the return was even better because I checked my competitiveness.

Later at lunch Chris invited us to stand on our chairs. Climbing on mine, I looked for my fellow swimmers. We nodded in acknowledgement of our earlier efforts. It made me feel good when everyone applauded for us. It didn't matter what order anyone placed. We were all thrilled with our accomplishment. A favorite poem by Marianne Williamson came to mind, "We are all meant to shine, as children do. It's not just in some of us, it's in everyone. And as we let our light shine, we unconsciously give other people permission to do the same."

I forgave myself. I could sparkle and support others at the same time. Sitting down, I hoped that I would carry this memory with me. I wanted to be a leader of our family and not get sucked into our old way of life back at home. After sitting, I reveled in my newfound understanding and the meal that was headed my way.

<u>"Where Every Day is a Holiday, and Every Meal a Feast!"</u>

· · ·

Oh, my goodness! It was my favorite meal. Wheeling their carts, staff wove around the thirty round tables and hundreds of chairs. When one arrived at our table, we received a platter of grilled cheese sandwiches and tureen of tomato soup with outstretched arms.

There may have been a better way to feed so many people, like buffet style, but this method brought families together. As tables took turns waiting for the server, we had time to speak to one another and to our new friends.

Earlier, Dave and I had discussed mealtimes. He told me he stuck to the family-style routine because studies showed when families ate together, the kids made healthier choices. And not only nutritionally, but they also performed better at school, took less risks, and had better table manners. I'm not so sure our behavior was modeling. We were often so hungry, we snatched chow with our hands and sometimes we laughed with full mouths. Conduct aside, it pleased me to see everyone's happy faces.

The data also stated everyone should help plan and cook, however in this environment, it wasn't feasible. There was an industrial kitchen and lots of cooks who tried to satisfy as many people as possible with their menus. For this to be accomplished, eating was simple. Bagels and waffles for breakfast, sandwiches and soup for lunch, and some type of meat and vegetables for dinner. A new addition was the salad bar. We had brought my mom's blueberries, along with a supply of nuts and seeds, and of course my coveted peanut butter. These items could round out any meal.

"Seeds and weeds, it's all you eat," Megan told me. My salad was coated with pumpkin seeds and walnuts when she made her statement. No one complained when I pulled out my extra-large tub of peanut butter. Spreading it on toast, making a quick sandwich, or even mixing it with salsa for the dinner fixings made everything taste better.

This, however, was one lunch I didn't need to add anything from my private stash: grilled cheese and tomato soup. This comfort lunch coincided with the swim. It warmed us after the chill of the water. Remembering this tradition, I had hoped for this very lunch. My wish came true!

"These are yummy," Michael said. He had a fistful of cheddar fish crackers that he shoved into his mouth.

"My fishes are swimming," Mia said.

"Me too," Megan chimed. They both dropped their crackers one at a time into their bowls.

"This is super simple," Mike said. "Cheese, bread, and lots of butter. Wiping his fingers on his napkin after taking a sandwich, his grease-stained fingerprints confirmed the sandwiches were greasy. Taking one, I broke off a chunk and dipped it into the steamy bowl. Cheese oozed from the crust. I soaked mine and then took a big bite.

"Yum! Such a splendid feast after my cold swim," I said.

"This is magnificent at any time," Mike said. I shared that when I was a teen camper, we called them greasy cheesies.

"Look at me." Mia scooped her fish crackers with a piece of crust.

"It looks like you're fishing," Megan said. She chased hers with a spoon, failing to catch one. Giving up, she pinched one between her fingers.

We had learned the former director, Todd, closed announcements by stating: At camp, every day is a holiday, and every meal is a feast! We started to say this to each other before we left the table, participating in this ritual.

Each spread was a celebration. We didn't have to plan, shop, or cook. Relishing one another's company, we dawdled instead of rushing away. Sure, we stacked dishes and sorted trash from compost. But, working together, all those hands made the cleaning go quickly. After indulging in my own second sandwich, I started to separate the silverware. I wasn't paying attention to announcements.

"Did you hear we're setting the campfire early, because it may rain?" Mike whispered. This was news to me, so I stopped and listened. Also, I didn't realize Mike was so interested in the skits. He hurried out of the dining room to my surprise. I wandered with the rest of the campers to the campfire circle.

·   ·   ·

<u>Campfire</u>

Normally held after dinner in the evening, the campfire was our final full camper gathering. Because of the threat of rain, everyone wanted to move the activity earlier in hope of avoiding the storm. I sat and waited for Mike to join me wondering why he had rushed off.

The skits started and each age group was included. We had seen the kids rehearsing the past few days and fed off their energy. Some of the sketches included our favorite staff members who knew how to "ham it up," and a few had parents who didn't mind being the brunt of the joke.

My favorite was when parent volunteers were given a brown bag containing a bandana. Dave explained that he was going to share a few uses of one.

"A bandana is a very good thing to have. Everyone on stage, get out your bandana, and I'll show you how useful it can be."

Describing all the ways a bandana could be used, the volunteers had to follow his instructions. Only the prop in the bottom of the bag was a banana–not a bandana. The participants tried to wipe the sweat off their face with a mushy banana. Fold it in half, wear on your head, and other ways that goo was smashed on them. Dave must have saved these bananas for days until they were more brown than yellow. The kids erupted in giggles.

There were a few adults who demonstrated their talents like piano playing and poetry reading. They were followed by tournament awards. Then to my surprise, Mike stood and walked to the stage. The emcee announced his act was a guitar solo. I knew he had taken lessons but was not aware he was good enough to play in front of the entire camp. I looked frantically to see who was going to wink at me and let me know I was being pranked. For a moment, I thought Mike had joined forces with Jenni. I thought, not cool, it was fine for kids to go and share their emerging talents, but an adult beginner! Agitated, my palms began to sweat with early-onset embarrassment.

Borrowing a guitar, he sat on a stool with a cowboy hat pulled low on his head, readied himself, and then strummed a few chords. He nodded to the emcee. A lone spotlight shone on Mike. A song with an infectious EDM beat by a band called Duck Sauce started playing. His head hung low like a country music performer, the crowd got into the layered beats and wondered what was going on. He didn't move an inch, nor play a single note. Suddenly, with perfect timing, he lifted his head to utter the song's only lyric: "Barbara Streisand." Mike had a goofy grin on his face because he knew he was spoofing everyone. The crowd loved it. But I didn't.

Shrinking in my chair, avoiding eye contact with anyone, I buried my face in my hands. Sensing him beside me, I looked his way.

"Really?" I said.

"What's wrong with you?"

"That's so embarrassing."

"What are you talking about?"

"I can't believe you would perform when you're not that good."

"Ouch! If you took a minute to look around, you'd see that everyone had fun."

I removed my hands from my face. He was right. Most kids knew the song and were in stiches. Others gave him a congratulatory clap on the back.

"That took courage for me to do that," he said. "Why wouldn't you support me?"

"I was embarrassed for you," I said.

"What?? That was fun; are you trying to ruin it?" he growled lowly, trying to not cause a scene.

I deserved his anger. I had taken my perspective that only children or experts should perform their sketch. Why did I buy into the idea that only stellar performances had to be shared on the stage? Allowing my discomfort over everyone watching him and then me for my reaction made me feel judged.

Why? There isn't judgment at camp. That was one of the reasons I had come to appreciate it. We were all doing our best and recognized it in one another.

"Oh my gosh, I'm so sorry!" I said.

Regaining himself and cutting me some slack, "I did it for fun, and I think it worked."

"Yup, I should have laughed along with the crowd."

Mike kissed me on the cheek. "All good, you pain in-the-*family camp*."

This was another *Ah-ha* moment. If I learned anything this week, it was that you couldn't read or schedule your family into success. You had to face all the moments with courage and love. During my runs, hikes, and milkshake conversations, I learned others had similar struggles. Mine was slowing down, loosening the reins, and finding balance. And guess what? I bet other people came to camp for their own reasons. I looked around. Everyone had something they hoped to gain. Even if it was only an escape from relying on technology. We were all perfectly imperfect. What a gift that I recognized this! And that Mike forgave me.

Campfire continued with more singing and then the most important tune of the evening, a closing song written by a former staffer. The lyrics spoke to how we would miss and crave camp after we departed for home.

Though many years and miles may come between us, there's a memory of a time that never ends, and as the days drift slowly by 'neath the sky, soon I'll be singing at camp with my friends.

Former staff stepped on stage, and we all swayed in time with them. As each verse was sung, we were closer to the campfire ending. This was the second time this week listening to a song moved me to tears. The first was at the initial sing-along when I heard my family singing "Mariah" and now this closing one. My heart pounded and hurt. I dug my fingernails into the palms of my hands to try and keep from crying. Searching for the kids, I found them in a huddle. Their scrunched faces told me all I needed to know; they were holding back tears, too.

We stayed after the last verse. Another one of those moments we didn't want to end. A quiet surrounded us as no one wanted to be the first to stir. I knew, even though we contemplated moving back to Arizona, and the logistics would be complicated, we were going to return to camp next year. How could I deny the kids? Mike? And myself? Mike's hand found mine and he gave it a squeeze. I leaned into him and sighed.

"Want to come back?" I asked.

"I already paid the deposit," he said.

"Let's go tell the kids," I said. I looked forward to being able to tell them the good news and seeing their frowns turn to smiles.

Hike to the Dam

We found the kids and after their shouts of joy, they asked us to go on the beaver dam hike with them. This was a once-in-a-lifetime opportunity. If we hurried, we could do it before the rain started. Plus, we had spent a lot of time with friends and other families, and this was an activity we could do together.

"How many beaver dams do you get to see in a lifetime?" I asked.

We saw a small gathering by the wishing well. "Hurry, slow pokes," Dave bellowed, "We need to do this before the rain."

Hustling, we gathered near him, and he said, "Wait until you see this place."

Following him past the snack bar, down the hill, and along the dam, we turned as if we were going to the springs.

"Did they build it at the springs?" Mike asked.

"Nah, we're going off trail," Dave said. "Look for clues." We all scanned the ground looking for signs of a beaver. Wood shavings? Bent over trees? I had no idea what to look for. My only beaver experience was Mr. Busy from *Lady and the Tramp*—the 1955 version when he gnaws off the muzzle from Lady's face.

"Is this a clue?" Michael asked. He stood beside a gnawed off tree branch.

"Yes!" Dave said. "Next, listen for trickling water." Trailing him, it was as if we were looking for the next bread crumb left by Hansel and Gretel. This section of forest was extremely dense. I strained to hear sounds of water.

"I don't hear anything, but I smell something familiar," I said.

"Smells like cookies," Mia said.

"Vanilla," Dave said. "Their marks smell like vanilla."

"Yummy," Megan said. "Since they found the first clues, does that mean they get vanilla shakes?" Everything always came back to milkshakes.

"If vanilla is their favorite," Dave winked.

"Impressive, Dave, you are a beaver expert, too?" Mike said.

"Well, the dam fascinated me, so I did a little research."

"What else did you learn?" I asked.

"Well, you may like this factoid."

"What?"

"They swim fast and can dive underwater for fifteen minutes to escape predators." He was right. (I was so curious about beavers after this hike that I went home and read a book on these little saviors. Check out the additional reading section at the end of this book if they intrigue you, too.)

"What animals prey on them?" Mike asked.

"Coyotes, wolves, and bears."

"Jeesh, I don't want to see any of those," I said.

Sliding in tight to Mike, I grabbed the girls' hands. This time I would protect them. Scanning the ground for animal scat, I concentrated so much on what poop I might see or who could be sneaking behind me, I bumped into Mike's back.

"Look!" he said. Suddenly, there was a clearing in the forest the size of a football field. The area was swamped. I saw a structure two feet high. The dozens of stumps we had passed on our way, the pines, dogwoods, and cottonwoods were intertwined to create the dam and a lodge. I was sure my jaw hung to the ground.

"How many beavers live in that mansion?" I asked.

"A mom and dad with a few kits."

"What are those bumps?" Megan asked.

"Those are the lodges, one is used for drying off, and the other is where they live."

"It must have taken a month to build, right?" Michael asked.

"A week, I read the entire beaver family works to create this sanctuary."

"Like us," Mike said. "Camp is our sanctuary."

"Many consider beavers to be pests, but they are really good for the environment."

"How so?" Megan asked.

"The ecosystems they build restore wetlands."

He looked at the gathered storm clouds. "Let's go, the dark sky looks fierce."

We retraced our path and walked back on the gravel road. Dashing the last few yards as rain started to pelt us, we popped into the snack bar. The kids went to get their free milkshake. Mike and I sat, staring at the downpour.

"Wasn't that neat?" Mia asked.

"Reminds me of us," I said.

"I'm not a rodent," Michael said. He chomped his teeth.

"Well, I meant we're both families trying to stay safe and warm."

"They have lodges," said Mia. "And we have snack bars."

"And both places have food!" Mike said. He leaned over and whispered in my ear, "The kids are eating shakes that smell like beaver butt."

"Shush, don't ruin it for them. I think they forgot what Dave told us."

Waiting out the storm, we watched it rage. Rain pelted the windows making it difficult to see. Lingering over the last bits of goodies in our cups, we scraped the bottoms until there was nothing left. We had to face it; the snack bar was closing, and we had to get to our cabin that was five hundred yards away.

"Now what?" I asked.

"Too bad this room doesn't lead to our cabin," Mike said. "Like the beaver lodge."

"We're going to get soaked," Michael said.

Mike stood and we followed him to the door. "I have an idea," he said. "Wait here."

Watching him walk into the driving rain, I couldn't imagine what he had in mind. He leaned against a patio table, lifted the outdoor umbrella out of the hole in the table, and untied it. Waving for us to come out, I saw it was wide enough to fit all of us underneath. We hooked arms. Steadying ourselves on the slippery walkway, we leaned on one another. The umbrella covered us, and we were protected.

"Thanks, honey," I said. "This was ingenious."

"Mom, I'm worried the storm will wash away the beaver dam," Mia said.

"Dave told us their structures are really sound," I said.

"And any damage will be fixed tonight by the entire clan," Mike added.

We stayed dry on our walk to our cabin. Entering on mine and Mike's side, we all crawled under the bedspread and snuggled. Mike cranked the heat and we dozed. Waking before the others, my heart burst lying next to those I loved most in the world. I thought about how our families have a lot in common with beaver families. We worked hard to make a safe home, feed everyone, and make time to play. There were storms in our lives, but with the help of one another we could weather them and be stronger for the effort.

Workshopping Our Stories

Eventually, I crawled out of bed to join John and Hope to workshop our pieces. I had missed the book club discussion but didn't mind as our cuddle time was more important. See? I had learned my lesson about too many activities and to focus on what was valuable. Reading my life essay, I was nervous. My hands shook and my voice quavered. After a few lines, my speech strengthened, and my fingers stopped shaking. Finishing, I smiled with relief. I had a voice, I wanted to be heard, and I had something to say. This session gave me the inspiration to keep going. The buried seed of longing was nourished.

Note: Once I returned home, I looked to nurture and grow my practice. My friend, Diane, mentioned she led a class called "Wise Women Write." One of my favorite quotes by Paulo Coelho, author of *The Alchemist*, came to mind. "And, when you want something, the entire universe conspires in helping you to achieve it." One session of meeting with three other women, fueled my need for more. Sharing our life essays and meeting once a month held us accountable. We inspired one another as we grew and learned.

Attending author events and learning this craft expanded my horizons and built my confidence. One morning, I found myself on a yoga mat seeking direction. My ask created space in my mind and heart. I met with Susan, my coach, shared my insight and we discussed next steps to start this writing journey. A list of memories, details, and meanings, (and several drafts!) led to this book. What started as an essay on childhood turned into another present camp had given me.

<u>Closing Ceremony</u>

. . .

The rain stopped after dinner, and it was time for closing events. Some folks went to watch the championship volleyball, others to the art show, and many to the snack bar for one last milkshake. Trying to squeeze in as much as possible, we passed some time at the match and then moved on to the craft room. Everyone's creations were displayed. Scattered on the shelves were sketches, watercolors, and ceramics. I found our fingerprint plate. It's wonderful, I thought. I'm going to use it every day, so we're reminded of our time here this summer.

After walking through twice and admiring everyone's creativity, I noticed Mike talking with Jenni and Scott. They wanted to get another milkshake. Discussing how cold it had become, I couldn't believe we would eat something to make us chilly. But it was our last chance. I shivered as I savored every bite of my final Peanut Butter Ripple. We heard the teens come back from their graveyard hike, and now we knew why the girls were so afraid.

The ritual was for some adults and staff to scare the teens. It wasn't too scary for them as they knew historically that the "big fright" would happen. They just didn't know when or where. Apparently, it happened at various times and places in the hike from year to year. This night, the adults hid behind the wide oak tree trunks on Chicken Hawk trail. Being the darkest and second spookiest spot (after the cemetery, of course), it was a prime location. They waited until all the teens were huddled in a tiny group. No one wanted to be on the edges of the pack. Then they sneaked up on them and shouted, "Boo!"

Note: Years later, I brought my wedding dress to donate to the camp costume closet. A young adult, Eric, or as we said "young professional" tried it on and it fit. Eric then wore it and came out of the lake near the graveyard. Our kids were teens that summer and they swore that they were the most scared they had ever been. It thrilled me that I had a little part in that plan.

After eavesdropping on the teens, I threw my cup away and glanced at the time. We were late for the closing ceremony. Pulling on our fleeces, we zipped them to our chins and cinched our hoodies. We hurried back to the fire circle. Dave had started speaking of joy. He wanted us to share our joyful moments with one another and then figure out how to reenact them at home. There was a ritual we could partake in. Passing a basket, he asked us to choose a smooth stone. It was to symbolize a moment we experienced joy during the week. Sharing, we worked our way around the circle. I told how Hope helped me realize we wanted to participate in Mike's *Name that Tune* challenge, because his enthusiasm and joy was contagious. After those who wanted a turn speaking were done, we walked to the edge of the water. Skipping our stones, we sent our stories into the world. We were to make space in our hearts for more.

This ceremony helped me to realize that families didn't just come here looking for something for themselves. They also came to support one another. We all had something to bring and something to give. I wanted to reflect more on this and add it to my list of values to bring home from camp. Adding what I thought the Warner family brought to camp to the list would make me happy. Already I recalled Mike's *Name That Tune* game, Mia on the playground taking care of toddlers, Megan being a student to the teen poker players, Michael taking care of his sisters in the creek, and me listening to Hope as she shared her workshop essay. I was positive there were many more examples.

Away from the heat of the flames, I shook from head to toe. I tucked my hands in my pockets and scrunched my toes together to try and find some warmth.

"Let's go back to the cottage and crank the heat," I said.

"Wait, I see the kids coming."

Joining us by the fire, we snuggled into each other for warmth. As we shared our favorite times, the clouds parted, and the twinkling stars reflected on the water. Leaving the fire, we approached the lake for a closer look. The millions of stars dancing on the smooth-as-glass water were dazzling.

"I've never seen this," I said. "Another new experience for me."

"It's as if all the beautiful camp moments culminated in the sky and are reflecting back to us," Mike said.

"It's pure magic," Michael said.

"Bye." Mia waved to the sparkly lake.

"See you later alligator." Megan waved.

Turning our backs, we were quiet as we walked away. There was nothing more to say.

SATURDAY AND DEPARTURE

<u>Omelets for breakfast</u>

Our last hours. The morning had the feel of each summer's last day before school started. We straggled into the dining hall for breakfast. Director Dave and Assistant Director Andrew made omelets. They had to be worn out from this busy week. Making the time to personally cook for us was the cherry on top of a fabulous week. Families came and went as the spread was more casual. There were no announcements, table call outs, or weather reports. There were hugs, tears, and vows to be back next year. Car keys were located, and vehicles driven from the parking lot. Crafts were gathered, suitcases packed, and farewells said.

"We don't want to leave." The kids dragged their feet on our walk to the cabin.

In the past we would have been too busy to share feelings. My desire to keep us on track meant focusing on the task at hand. This time, I asked them to share why.

"I'm going to miss being outside," Megan said.

"I wish I could take all my new friends home with me," Mia said.

"I won't see Andy and Maria for a whole year," Mike added.

"Well, let's talk about all that on the car ride," Mike said. What a great idea! We could give them ownership of how to stay in touch with their friends and how to make time to explore outside. They could help me add to my list of ways to practice family camp at home.

It was time. We were ready.

I swept the floors of the cabin as I wanted to leave it as we found it. I took some deep breaths and thanked the cabin for keeping us warm and cozy during the week. I swear it seemed as if it was only yesterday when I had held the broom upon our arrival. Placing it in the closet, I turned for one more look. After admiring how clean we were leaving it for the next family, I said a little prayer. I hoped their week was as gratifying as ours. Then I left Mike and the kids to pack everything as I had one more to-do item.

"Meet me in twenty minutes at the playground?" I asked.

· · ·

<u>The Swing is my Special Place</u>

I had the playground to myself. All was silenced. Everyone else had packed, cleaned their cabins, and were on their drive home.

The speed boat sat idled, no bocce balls clanged, no friends called for a milkshake, and the gaga pit, (the fenced in ball game area that hummed with activity all week), was emptied of children. The stillness was perhaps more important than all the noises of fun and enjoyment. I was at peace.

Sitting in my favorite swing, I twisted back and forth. I dragged my bare feet in the cool sand. Reflecting on the week, I captured this emotional state of satisfaction to carry in my heart. At home I would recall this moment whenever I needed a sense of contentment.

I had not told anyone the swing set was my special place. Not even Mike. It's not that I thought he wouldn't understand. This was one of those things I wanted to keep private. When I was a teen camper and got overwhelmed with all the togetherness, I would sneak down here. Usually at night, I sat and pumped my legs harder and lifted higher. It's as if I reached for the stars and their stillness. This motion and time to myself always settled me.

I never made this connection, but now as a mother I recognized I leaned on swings a lot. Using a portable swing for the kids when they were babies was a no brainer. It always worked at either lulling them to sleep or soothing them when they were fussy. Plus, it was a safe place for them. How funny, I mused how I never gave up this practice. Was I looking for the same state of serenity for myself? Maybe.

Mike pulled the minivan around and gave a light tap on the horn. I peeled myself away and turned my back on the lake. The kids were in the car. We're packed and ready to go, but we were having a hard time leaving. We all have fiddled the morning away trying to extend our stay. Mike in conversations over breakfast, the kids dawdled while packing their bags, and me on the playground.

Slowly, we drove out of camp. But wait, I lied, we had one more stop. Swinging by Jenni's cabin we blasted the horn at her. Hers was the last family to leave as she had some extra packing. She was partially hidden behind the bloomers and onesies that I hung on her clothing line. I had found some vintage underwear in the staff wardrobe closet and borrowed them to give her a giggle. I'd have to remember to tell her that it was Scott that gave me the idea.

Laughing over how her cabin was on the way out of camp in a primo viewing spot, I grinned. I had much to look forward to until our return. I get to practice all that I've learned about myself, Mike, and the kids. How to check my ego and to quit worrying about the future. Hoping to bring family camp values home to our community, I thought of how I needed to extend myself to my running community. How not to get swayed from our new rituals like family mealtime, playing cards, or exploring new activities. This was the first time in a long while that I looked forward to planning. But, now how I wanted us to be–versus organizing a to- do list of things we needed to accomplish.

The kids slept. They had cried a few tears like my siblings and I had all those years ago when we left camp. Mike scanned the stereo trying to find music. I closed my eyes, put myself back on that swing, and pumped my legs in my mind. I suppose this was how life was going to be for me and us. A back-and-forth tussle I would contend with forever. I had forgiven myself for losing my way.

And yet, I wondered if the camp spirit would work its magic on us the rest of the year. I wanted to make sure that I and the family didn't slip back into negative traits and kept focused on these positive behaviors that were being reinforced.

Mike quit looking for a static free station and turned off the radio. So, I sang a few bars of the final closing camp song.

Though many years and miles may come between us
There's a memory of a time that never ends,
And as the days drift slowly by 'neath the Pennsylvania sky
I'm singing at Deer Valley with my friends

The lyrics reminded me that we had paid our deposit and would return in 357 days. We would do our best at home to work on being a loving family focused on meaningful values. Camp and our community would be there for us for a reset if we needed it.

REFLECTIONS

Megan

When my mom asked me to write a reflection for her camp book, it was no surprise I was excited. But sitting and trying to write was difficult, because camp seriously holds all my biggest and best memories. It reminds me of an ex-staff quote I had heard: "You have created more memories than most people will have in a lifetime."

Here I am, a twenty-five-year-old kid-at-heart starting out her career in Hawaii in wilderness therapy, reminiscing about how I got here and what I value in life. So, my story will be a reflection, sprinkled with a few memories.

YMCA Family Camp is home to me. I spent every summer there since I was seven years old as a camper.

In high school, I volunteered for five weeks grinding away in the kitchen, and I spent three summers on staff in my college years. Camp exposed me to that last childhood in the woods. I grew up riding horses and playing robber to "steal" ice cream from the snack bar, catching crayfish in the creek, and building complex structures to drop eggs from the Mount Davis tower.

My most trusted friends to this day all come from camp. I fell in love at camp. I have buddies on nearly every continent from working with the international staff. I developed a realization that a family can be found anywhere you go. Camp was the root of my life-long passion for sustainability and outdoor education. Giving me a sense of belonging and awareness, I knew I was going to take my college degree straight into the woods.

Camp was also wonderful in how grungy it could be —getting seventy mosquito bites, eating the same seven meals for eleven weeks as a staff member, and getting excited to forage for food at the local gas station. Working fifteen-hour workdays, I then stayed awake until 2:00 a.m. swapping kid stories, playing in mud, and being one of thirty staff members to lose your voice.

Some of my fondest memories were being encouraged by a close friend to sing "Geronimo" on stage for the first time, playing zombie apocalypse capture-the-flag in the dark and becoming a teens counselor. And if those weren't enough, I gathered one hundred people on the beach to do a squat challenge, taught my high school volunteers leadership lessons in my featured 'Motivation Monday with Meg,' watched a young teen endure an egg drop that plopped directly on her head (only to laugh and roll down the big hill shortly after), and played quidditch. All of these led to hearing the teens reflect how camp helped them with bullying, anxiety, and depression. And lastly, ugly crying from singing our farewell song on Friday evening.

Family camp also gave me a strong value system. As staff members, we were always reminded of the motto "I Am Third," meaning your worldviews come first, others come second, and you are third. I constantly experienced a community of people who went out of their way to make someone's day, every day. Camp is where I experienced my daily dose of kindness from saying hello to everyone I passed to having a phantom friend send me on an elaborate scavenger hunt to encounter all the animals I love. But, best of all, having all your campers bring you compliments and dress you like a princess because that was one of your childhood dreams.

<u>Mia</u>

When I think back on my first summer at camp, I remember the jungle gym. I had spent the whole week with two girls playing make believe on the jungle gym by the lakefront beach. All I wanted to do was spend time with my friends and suspend myself in a utopia. As I got older and my friend group grew, I realized the jungle gym wasn't my utopia, camp was. Camp suspends real life and allows you to disconnect from society so you can connect with the community around you. It took me a decade of being a camper, three years working on staff, and a volunteer trip to Honduras with other campers to realize that camp was more than a vacation.

The summer going into my sophomore year of high school I had learned about the Salt (Service and Leadership Training) and Clipper (Camp Leadership Instructional Program) programs. I begged my mom and dad to let me be a SALT that summer. Little did we know my one-week would turn into a month and a half.

I spent two weeks working in the kitchen serving food, developing friendships with coworkers who live across the globe, and building relationships with campers from different weeks. I asked my supervisor if I could stay for another two weeks. I ended up spending an entire month working at camp under their service and leadership training program. It was one of the best summers of my life, and my first time away from home. I learned a lot about myself and how I can keep going no matter how tired I was. I also learned how much effort goes into making camp a special experience for anyone who drives through the front entrance.

I was hooked. The next summer I worked for three weeks, and the summer after I worked another three weeks. I learned that as much as adults are role models to me, I was at an age to be a role model to others. I remember one summer we teens decided to join in a game of Ga-Ga with the younger kids (note: Ga-Ga is dodgeball but played in a wood-fenced pen). It wasn't until a nine-year-old Jack yelled, "Get Mia and Megan out! We can't have them beating us!" that Megan and I realized they knew who we were. We had never told them our names, and yet they knew. We were role models without even realizing it. It took me back to a time when I looked at the teens at camp and wanted to do what they were doing. As I was excited that I was now a teen being able to do what they had done, I never took a second to realize there were little Mia's running around camp waiting to be able to do what I was doing.

Camp guided me through all my transitions of childhood into my young professional self. It was in my senior year of university that camp came full circle. My father had always gone to Morning Watch and tried to get me to join. Being a teenager, I was too tired after staying awake 'till 2:00 a.m. hanging out with my friends to wake and go. That year I had decided I would give it a go and maybe sneak off for a cheeky little nap afterwards. Being able to hear other adults talk about their day-to-day battles and how they work through them really opened my eyes to the fact I am not alone. I had developed anxiety and the time with these adults helped me. It also showed me I can bring a unique perspective to the group. It taught me my voice matters, and there are people out there wanting to listen and help.

At the last Morning Watch, we talked about the trapeze. How you must have the confidence to jump, the strength to hold on while you swing across your obstacle, and the faith that someone was on the other end to catch you. Not only did we discuss what it means to be the person swinging, I shared the perspective of the person on the other end being there to catch the person coming towards you. How sometimes the person may not want to jump and when is it okay to walk away from being ready to catch them. I believe after this specific Morning Watch, it not only brought my father and me closer, but it also brought a lot of other parents at camp closer to me.

That evening the teens all stayed awake as late as possible. My buddies and I had been wandering around camp taking in our last moments when we stumbled upon them struggling to stay awake. These nights were my favorite. We would get vulnerable with one another and open about the struggles with friends and family we had had over the past year. I talked with this one girl who was struggling with her friends. I think I gave her some fantastic advice about opening to a person who hurt you and telling them why. A vulnerable conversation can lead to the most open and honest relationship.

The next morning, they stayed around the cafeteria saying their goodbyes until next year. Her father approached me to say he was grateful for the advice I gave his daughter because she really needed the guidance, and how he was glad she was able to get it from me. I had a couple parents whom I had gotten to really know throughout the week letting me know they're a phone call away. And tell me that they're happy to have watched me grow these past years. That week at camp really showed me how much I had grown over the decades of camping, and how unity is truly built at this YMCA family camp.

Michael

There is no singular story that does justice to the experience of family camp. Hell, if you have read this far you already know (based upon word count alone). Therefore, it is not an easy task to boil down my personal history. Perhaps I should write my own book. The bottom line is, as I look through old camp photos, I am reminded not only of the irreplaceable memories from within the campgrounds, but more so of the friendships I am able to maintain to this day— extending beyond the woods. Family camp gave me the capability to spread roots throughout the country and form a bond with co-campers and staff members that is unaffected by time or distance.

When we changed to camping week 0, it was no different than moving towns. I found myself in a scenario where the buddies I had the previous year wouldn't be there. Time to make new ones and new memories! What my eleven-year-old self didn't know was that for years I would be visiting camp buddies when my family traveled to my grandparents for holidays. My younger self had no clue that eight years after meeting him at camp, I would travel to Texas to see one of my best friends graduate high school. I can say eight years of friendship, but the truth of the matter is we only ever saw each other for a total of eight weeks over fifteen years. But in those weeks at camp were hours of playing, capturing the flag, learning to sail, playing cards, and somehow fitting more than thirty hours' worth of entertainment into a single day—for seven days straight. All the bonding compressed into such a small window was a guarantee for lifelong friendships.

In my final years of high school, I volunteered to work at camp in small sessions. This was a big commitment (flying across the country and residing in Pennsylvania for months during the summer), but same as before, I knew it meant new pals and memories. I was matched with campers from other weeks who were volunteering as well and even though we didn't know each other, we all knew "camp." That's all it takes. While camp has a different meaning to each person, we understand what camp means to everyone. When you set out with the common goal to provide and build upon the excellent experience you were fortunate to receive as a camper, you flourish as a staff.

When I joined the staff after my freshman year of college, I knew I would be working harder than I had ever worked before. But it felt like stealing. There is no amount of effort you can put into family camp to pay back the rewards you have received. As a staff one summer, we shared that mindset. I cannot stress how quickly true relationships formed in only thirteen weeks on staff. Those of us not so sleep dependent stayed awake for hours after programs ended for the evening, forming the Late-Night Crew. Between midnight runs to Sheetz for fried Mac-N-

Cheese bites, playing cards, or delving into topics of the theoretical in the lobby of the staff lodge, I grew to appreciate so many of the unique personalities I was serving with. Because of my friendships built through being a staff member, I have traveled the country sight-seeing, attended sporting events with on-field passes, served as a groomsman in a wedding, and had many road trips.

So, while I may not be able to visit family camp as often as I would like, because of the bonds it has granted to me, the magic lives on in the world beyond the campground.

. . .

<u>Maria</u>

I have more to say! I have so many memories and tried to include them all. If you have camped with me, please forgive me for not writing about you or your favorite activity. There is so much more to camp than I've included.

When it came time to sit and write, my family helped to review my list of memories. If you attend a family camp, why not take some time to write your moments and create your own list? (See the journaling prompts at the end to get started! Or a writing workshop weekend at camp?) If you don't attend camp, I bet you have some stories you cherish and could record.

It took years of writing to flesh out these stories and their importance. I did not recognize how meaningful they were to me until I put pen to paper. While my children were younger, I was often overwhelmed with motherhood. My goal pre-camp was to create a storybook life and family. I wish I could go back in time and tell my younger self to stop trying to be flawless and be herself. Being myself was enough! A gratitude practice and writing this memoir aided me in uncovering my good fortune and happiness to have this time with my husband and children for one week every summer.

I'm grateful for every moment and all the staff, campers, volunteers, board members, etc. that work so hard to make camp fabulous!

My (maybe) final word: I love what camp means to everyone and that we come together once a year to keep this tradition alive!

<u>Mike</u>

Oh, good gracious! How to reflect on sixteen years of amazing experiences, the maturing of our children, and my own personal growth all within a few paragraphs? This likely is a challenging task for a highly accomplished writer, which I am certainly not. But when Maria asked for the kids and me to each take a stab at it, I figured that penning a few words about our beloved family camp shouldn't be too tough.

Like many of our fondest memories, heading off to our first year at camp seems like a lifetime ago and just yesterday, at the same time. Looking back now, I still cannot believe that we took ten days out of every single year, to fly across the country, load up a rented minivan with luggage, bedding, towels, bikes, fishing gear, and an array of other sporting goods and then travel back in time to spend a week in a spartan cabin, sleeping on wire & vinyl mattresses. Well, we did. Yet each and every year, driving back to civilization, we all could not wait for fifty-one weeks to pass.

Since every day at camp generated dozens of experiences and memories, how do I summarize 2,200 of these vignettes? I like the power of three's, so I'll break down my thoughts and reflections into three phases. For the first two years, I attacked every single day like a maniac. We didn't really know anyone yet, so I focused on reliving my youth, satiating my need for competition, and spending time with Maria and the kids after their group activities. I signed up for almost every competition: volleyball, bocce, ping-pong, cards, sailing, etc. Each day, waking early before my family woke, I'd quietly slip out to fish, jog, bird watch, or bike. We'd grab breakfast together before the kids went off with their age groups, and then I would go back to running on high. I would go on an advanced horse ride through forest trails, zip over to join my team volleyball match, jog around the lake with Maria, play a round of bocci, and start a project in the craft shop all before noon. We'd stuff our faces at lunch, listen to the kids excitedly share their morning stories, and then go do five more things in the afternoon. I could not get enough. Dinner, then crafts or a long walk or a pontoon ride, ice cream or smores, and then we'd conk out for the night. Tomorrow: wash, rinse, and repeat. We were hooked!

As these early years progressed, my appreciation of the tradition my wife talked us into grew. Strong friendships with some of the other families developed, and the kids started keeping in touch with friends all year around. I went from going to a few Morning Watches each week, to loving the spiritual immersion each and every day. A familiarity with camp leadership developed and then grew into friendships themselves. Participation in competitions morphed from a desire to win into just being part of everything. Note: this does not apply to Race Day on the water, where competing to win on the JY-class sailboats is and always has been an absolute focus. Case in point: My good friend, Hunter, permanently kicked me off his "crew" (it's a two-person crew) and didn't speak to me for the rest of week because I chose a poor tack, costing us the lead with only a quarter mile to go. And yes, I totally understood!

The third phase hit by around year six or seven. We had become "The Warner Family," where almost all 300 campers and 40 staffers knew us, save for newcomers. Each year became more and more like returning home. A home that you only spend one week in, out of fifty-two. Year round, our children's thoughts were never far from camp and casual conversation with them frequently reflected back on an experience or refer-enced excitement of the year to come. Maria and I drew closer. Our friendship with other parents strengthened. When one of my many minor injuries led to a hospital visit, another couple took me there, underscoring the family in Family Camp. Our kids were growing up, each of them planning on the staff roles they would enjoy most, when they earned their spot. For me, the habit of Morning Watch turned into a passion, which I would reflect on all year and still do. My focus for these last seven or eight years was to make the most of every moment, stay up as late as possible, and connect with as many people as I could. Once our children became junior staff volunteers and then full staff members, the pride Maria and I experienced from parents telling us what wonderful young adults we raised is still the icing on one huge sheet cake. Cake! Cake! Cake! (Reference: anyone with a birthday had 300 family member sing to them after dinner, ending in a loud chant for cake.) A grown man of fifty-seven, and I'm literally fighting off tears of joy as I am finishing these reflections. I lost. Thank you for reading.

Oh, wait, on a final note: I was the one who was out in front at the triathlon finish and slowed to let Maria cross with me. Just wanted to set the (family camp) story straight! :)

DAD'S FUNERAL (IN CASE YOU WERE WONDERING)

Mom invited a few families we had camped with all those decades ago to join us in our celebration of his life. Afterwards we gathered for a picnic, like BBQ night at camp. Mom asked our fellow camp friends to lead us in song, choosing "Johnny Appleseed" for grace. And guess what? It rained!

Every time I sat to write; I was reminded of not only all the happy moments but the sadness of my father's passing. For he genuinely loved camp and was grateful to help us have this experience every summer. I hoped he died knowing deep down he made a difference in our lives by working to take us to camp each year.

Revisiting camp in my writing was soothing to my soul. Every recollection is a reminder of an earlier time in my life. When I take all the fun times, scary moments, chances to grow, and view them from afar, it reminds me that this is what being human is all about.

ADDITIONAL READING LIST

Feiler, Bruce, *The Secrets of Happy Families*, New York, HarperCollins Publishers, 2013.

Goldfarb, Ben, *Eager Beavers Matter*, White River Junction VT, Chelsea Green Publishing, 2018.

Kenison, Katrina, *The Gift of an Ordinary Day: A Mother's Memoir*, New York, Grand Central Publishing a division of Hachette Book Group, Inc., 2009.

Li, Qing, *Forest Bathing*, Newbury Port, MA, Conari Press an Imprint of Red Wheel/Weiser, LLC, 2018.

Louv, Richard, *Last Child in the Woods*, Chapel Hill, Algonquin Books of Chapel Hill a division of Workman Publishing, 2005, 2008.

Monke, Audrey, *Happy Campers*, New York, Hachette Book Group, 2019.

Sorenson, Jacob, *Sacred Playgrounds*, Eugene,

Cascade Books an Imprint of Wipf and Stock Publishers, 2021.

Williams, Florence, *The Nature Fix*, New York, W.W. Norton & Company, Inc., 2017.

ALLIANCE CONSULTING
EMPLOYEES THAT PERISHED ON
9/11

Eric Bennett
Kenny Caldwell
Laura Giglio
Roland Pacheco
Larry Senko
Felicia Traylor-Bass
Melissa Vincent

MARIA'S FAMILY CAMP
VALUES LIST

Nostalgia is important in remembering your loved ones
Practice gratitude
Dine with friends and family
Make new friends
Chores are good for everyone
Family time is key
Try new activities
Recognize traditions
Make time for play
Build a community
Fun with harmless pranks
Couple time
Allow kids some slack
Have a respect for nature
Encourage & praise one another
Be goofy and silly
Support everyone

Learn about everyone

More fun with harmless pranks

Catch your kids doing something good

Spirituality of nature

Success is if your kids talk about you in an excellent way

Cook/feed others

Picnic

Play games where everyone wins

Recognize and share your blessings

Trust your kids (but verify)

Practice cooperation

Patriotism

Marriage is a team

Importance of being a human being and not a human doing

Check your competitiveness—when appropriate

Appreciate the simple

Revel in others silliness

Marvel at nature

Get outside more

Importance of reflection

Recognizing the magic in the moments

Serving

Having a special place

Be kind

Be a student and a teacher

WARNER FAMILY FAVORITE CAMP SAYINGS

No purpling (no blue-boys and red-girls to be alone as a couple)

You can sleep when you're dead. (FOMO)

Every day is a holiday, and every meal is a feast. (said by Todd Brinkman at announcements)

FAMILY CAMP! (in lieu of swearing)

Want to get a milkshake? (enough said)

Young professionals (college age and older that needed their own age group)

You have had more memories than most people will have in a lifetime.

I'm too drunk to taste this chicken. (Inappropriate movie quote when Michael introduced himself to campers as a staff member at Town Hall-YIKES!)

From the outside looking in, you can't understand it, and from the inside looking out, you can't explain it. (I hope I've done a decent job with this book)

Poop before group. (I think this is the kids' saying from when they were on staff and very busy with lots of responsibilities.)

The week is going by too fast. (me on the way in the entrance on the first day)

Returning to camp is like going to a family reunion with 300 family members you want to spend time with. (How Mike describes camp to everyone.)

Chanting makes it right. (Staff saying?)

JOURNALING PROMPTS

1. Does your family have a traditional vacation spot? Describe who started the tradition, where it is located, and the meaning to your family.
2. Is there a historical moment in your life, like 9/11, that triggered reflection/reset for you?
3. How is your current family life different than your childhood home?
4. Are there activities that your family experiences together outside? Describe them here. (cloud gazing, four leaf clover searching, watching the sunset, etc.)
5. Does your family have favorite songs? Sayings? Meals? Snacks?
6. How does technology/social media impact your family? Do you have rules around no-tech meals or Sundays as tech-free days?

7. What are ways that your family practices gratitude?
8. Can you think of some chores that you can make more fun for the family?
9. List the ways that you can give of time/talent/treasure to your community? (church, neighborhood, school)
10. List the activities that you would like to make time for.
11. List the activities that you would like your family to let go of.
12. Did you ever volunteer or work at a camp? How did that experience impact you as an adult?
13. Did you make a camp bestie? Describe that friendship.
14. List any encounters you've had with wildlife that you could learn from.
15. What lessons have your children taught you?
16. Does your family practice blessings? How have you been blessed in your life?
17. Any long-lost childhood dream that you would like to revisit?
18. Ways that your family is strong and resilient?
19. What ways can you support other families?
20. Do you have family values? List them.

ABOUT THE AUTHOR

Maria Warner grew up in Penn Hills, PA. She graduated with a B.A. in Business Administration and Political Science from The University of Pittsburgh. Maria has also lived in Florida, Michigan, Toronto, New Jersey, and currently resides in Arizona. She never lost her love for the Pennsylvania wilderness. In addition to being a writer, Maria's daily practices include meditation, reading, and being in nature.